FROM FATHER TO SON

FROM FATHER
TO SON

The letters of Captain Eddie Rickenbacker

to his son William,

from boyhood to manhood

★ ★ ★

Edited, with notes and introduction,

by William F. Rickenbacker

WALKER AND COMPANY / New York

First published in the United States of America in 1970 by the Walker Publishing Company, Inc.

Published simultaneously in Canada by The Ryerson Press, Toronto.

Library of Congress Catalog Card Number: 78-126110

Printed in the United States of America.

ISBN: 0-8027-0325-9

Book designed by Lena Fong Hor

To my wonderful sons
JAMES
and
THOMAS
As these priceless letters
were once dedicated to me
so I now rededicate them
with love proudly to you

Introduction

This remarkable series of letters from a busy father to an increasingly busy son covers a period of almost thirty years—from 1937 to 1965. The first letter is written from a world-famous man of forty-seven to a boy of nine. The last letter is from a man of seventy-five to his son of thirty-seven. Throughout the series, only a portion of which is published here, there breathes the very essence of my father as those of us who are close to him know him: generosity, compassion, extraordinary realism, energy, the infinite security of settled opinion amazingly mingled with tolerance and exquisite diplomacy—but I will let you meet him for yourself.

A word is in order about the conditions that gave rise to these letters. After all, most boys of nine don't receive letters from their parents at all, because if there's anything to be said it will be said at the dinner table. This boy of nine was away at school every year, September through June, from 1937 until 1949. He was home for eighteen months and then away again in the military service. Even if he had been home, he would not have seen too much of his father, for the world knows that Captain Eddie Rickenbacker has stayed on the move. The letters keep up their intensity and frequency until 1955, when the boy is finally out of the military service, married, and settled down in New York City with his father and mother and eight million other good people for neighbors. At long last there is no need for letters any more.

Dad's letters show that it clearly was not a one-sided correspondence. There exists—as the last letter in this series indicates—a whole collection of my letters to my parents during these same years, hundreds of them, in typewriter, pencil, and pen, raising the normal questions and inviting the normal bruises of youth and adolescence and maturity. Perhaps my sons will want to read them. Their chief virtue is that they called forth the magnificence of Dad's responses.

You might say we have here an architectural design for a bridge to get over the "generation gap." Fathers and sons have had difficulty talking with each other for the last five or six thousand years, but the difficulty can melt away when father and son have sufficient honesty and patience and a will to meet. Those are rare commodities in any age, and I was blessed with a father who showered them in all directions.

Dad's letters were a powerful influence on me, but it is worth mentioning that they couldn't have exerted such an influence if it hadn't been for Mother. She was always there to pick up the pieces, as it were—for she also answered every letter I ever wrote—and while Dad was free as a bird to instruct me in the arts of politics and war and aviation and diplomacy, he could count on Mother to remember to tell me to bring the overcoat home, and the ration stamps for red meat during the war, and who said what to whom. Dad's letters are strong medicine and iron bracing. Luckily I didn't exist on them alone. There was always the warm and chatty domestic news roundup from this very remarkable woman. God bless her for every sweet and loving word she ever wrote!

Looking through the letters, I am struck by the recurring resolve on the part of both father and son to become pure in heart by giving up booze. Why not? I mention it in order to avoid misunderstanding: we are not a family of drunkards. We are people who enjoy life and work hard and play hard and make grandiose resolutions, like most people. Neither of us has had a smoke for many years. I haven't had a drink for going on three years. And we're all just as sweet-tempered as ever.

The "Sheppy" you will meet in these letters is the gentle Marguerite H. Shepherd who has been Dad's secretary and administrative assistant since 1923, and who is as much a member of the family as I am. There is simply no way to calculate what we all owe to her, but I have the comfort of my faith that such accounts are accurately maintained in Heaven.

I have Dad's gracious permission to publish these letters. The excerpts given here are selected because of their general historical interest or because of their personal and inspirational force. One of my dreams is that this book will be of value to other fathers and other sons.

In six or seven places I have touched up an obvious typographical error or spelled a word in accordance with more recent practice. Otherwise you see the letters much as I saw them when they unfolded out of their envelopes in Tarrytown and Bronxville and New York and Asheville and Cambridge, San Antonio and Los Angeles and Seoul and Lubbock—neatly typed on the stationery of the Office of the President of Eastern Air Lines and signed "Daddy."

Those princely donations of spirit deserve to be shared as widely as possible.

W. F. R.

Briarcliff Manor, New York
April 1970

PHOTO 1: The Rickenbacker family, in Bronxville, N.Y.
William is at right, David at left.

PHOTO 2: A trip West in 1938. Captain Eddie with Bill and Dale Chambers, nephew of World War I ace Reed Chambers; in Arizona (*above*).

PHOTO 3: Father and son on a brief side trip to Mexico (*below*).

PHOTO 4: The former chief at Indianapolis takes his sons back to the Speedway in 1939.

PHOTO 5: Soldier's Vodka from the Russian tour, 1942. A staged photograph to be sent to the Russian general who gave the vodka to Captain Eddie.

PHOTO 6: The June 11, 1951 New York Daily *News* caption read "Chip Off the Old Rick: Capt. Eddie Rickenbacker, famed World War I ace, swears his son William, 22, into the Air Force as an aviation cadet at 39 Whitehall."

PHOTO 7: February 9, 1952. Reese Air Force Base. Bill gets his wings.

FROM FATHER TO SON

BOYHOOD

★　　★　　★

1937-1945

In April of 1937 the General Manager of Eastern Air Lines addresses a letter to his nine-year-old son at home. Like almost all of the more than two hundred letters that were to follow over the years, its thrust was toward the future.

1775 Broadway
April 13, 1937

My dear Pal Billy:

This letter has gone from San Francisco to Hong Kong, China, and return on the first through flight connecting the Orient with the United States by the Pan American Airways China Clipper.

As a first cover it will become invaluable. As a keepsake it will be a remembrance of your Daddy's interest in the progress of aviation for your benefit, and I hope will be appreciated.

It will be interesting to you to know that instead of taking three weeks by boat to get from San Francisco to Hong Kong, China, the China Clipper will cover this same distance in less than seven days and, in my opinion, when you have grown up in the next twenty-five years, it will be done in from twenty to twenty-five hours through the stratosphere.

Keep this letter for its future value.

With love,

Daddy

Master Billy Rickenbacker
8 Prescott Avenue
Bronxville, N.Y.

By the autumn of 1937 the family was split up. My older brother Dave was away at school in Arizona and I was away at school in Tarrytown, New York. Dad began to solve the communications problem with regular letters of advice, encouragement, personal anecdote, glimpses of the future. And now commences also the long-term effort to get the scattered brood to keep in touch.

4

July 6, 1939

My dear Pal Bill:

This first cover inaugurating the autogiro mail service from the roof of the Philadelphia Post Office to Camden Airport will become known as one of the epochal events of air transportation.

It is your Dad's good fortune to be President of Eastern Air Lines, which will operate this service—the first of its kind anywhere in the world.

As time goes on I prophesy that all large cities will have shuttle service by the autogiro from the main airport to the roof of the main post office.

Further, this will be a stepping stone to the development of the helicopter which will be used for pick-up and delivery of mail, passengers and express in all large communities between the suburbs and the main airport, increasing the speed of delivery and travel tremendously.

You and Brother David I hope some day will become part of the results of your Dad's pioneering efforts.

Love,

Daddy

Master William Rickenbacker
130 East End Avenue
New York, N.Y.

The collection of first covers grew over the years until it numbered in the hundreds. It filled an entire suitcase. In one of our many moves, the suitcase disappeared. Nevertheless we received quite an education in the development of air transportation along the way. Clearly Dad was looking forward to having his sons join him in his business. Autogiros and helicopters never became a major form of transportation, but their first cousin, the STOL craft, will some day do the job Dad envisioned for the autogiro.

★   ★   ★

1775 Broadway
February 7, 1939

My dear Pal Bill:

I was surprised to note from your January report card that you had failed to make the honor list because of your missing out on American history.

Gosh—with all your knowledge of American

history and the great amount of traveling you have done, this should be one of your best subjects.

This letter is not meant to censure you for your failure, but to encourage you to take advantage of your knowledge and ability as a student by simply applying yourself to your studies a little more thoroughly.

You know how badly Mother and I want you to be on the honor roll and unless you can be, I am afraid I am going to have to hold off buying you a new set of golf clubs, which I dislike doing very much as I want you to have them.

However, at the same time, I want you to realize how hard I have to work to get the money to buy them, and to show your appreciation by being the type of young man we can all be proud of. You have it in you and I know you can do it.

With love,

As ever,

Daddy

Master Billy Rickenbacker
The Irving School
Tarrytown-on-Hudson, N.Y.

My dear Pal Bill:

I came across the following quotation a few days ago by Dale Carnegie which, in my opinion, is of utmost value to boys of your age:

"H. Gordon Selfridge, proprietor of the famous Selfridge's store in London, one day called the department heads of his store together to discuss the qualities of leadership. He gave them a leaflet he had written on the subject. Here it is:

"The Boss drives his men; the Leader coaches them.
The Boss depends on authority; the Leader on good will.
The Boss inspires fear; the Leader inspires enthusiasm.
The Boss says 'I'; the Leader says 'we.'
The Boss says 'get there on time'; the Leader gets there ahead of time.
The Boss fixes the blame for the breakdown; the Leader fixes the breakdown.
The Boss knows how it is done; the Leader shows how.

The Boss makes work a drudgery; the Leader makes work a game.

The Boss says 'go!' The Leader says 'Let's go!' "

You remember well having seen the mammoth Selfridge store in London. With a leader who understands true problems of leadership such as is shown, we can well understand how this mammoth department store grew from nothing into one of the world's largest.

Keep this letter always before you and try to memorize and understand each quotation, in order that you, too, may prepare yourself for the quality of leadership that all men hope for.

Love,

Daddy

Wm. F. Rickenbacker
The Asheville School
Asheville, North Carolina

My dear Pal Bill:

I read your letter last evening and reread it several times. I know you will accept my suggestions as advice instead of criticism because you are entirely too fine a boy to let little things worry you as intimated and stated in your letter as to what some of the boys seem to be doing with the hope of getting your goat.

There is nothing new in boys being mischievous and picking on one another. Join in with them and make them like you for what you are, and still you will have no difficulty in being a little gentleman. If they want to be mischievous, you be the same.

I say boys have a habit of picking on one another. I often think of my own youth when all the kids used to call me "Dutchy," simply because I had a German name, and "Towhead," because I had white hair. They used to make me so mad I could see stars, but as I look back on it now all I should have done was to admit that I was what they called me and laugh it off.

By so doing, you take the wind out of their sails and they have nothing to follow through with and it does not hurt you, but if you get mad they immediately think they are cute and smart, and continue.

Just think what a freckle-faced, red-headed boy has to contend with. They are always being picked on by their friends, acquaintances and school mates, criticized and abused. They have to learn how to take it, and that is one of the reasons why these red-headed boys grow up into red-headed men and usually prove to be a great success in some line of endeavor or another.

You can take it with a smile I know and never let them get your goat.

I am delighted to hear of the progress you are making at the school, and I feel sure within a few months you will be up there at the top of the class, and happy as a lark, as I am sincerely interested in your being so.

With love,

Daddy

★   ★   ★

Encouragement, encouragement! An eleven-year-old boy who thinks he has a long way to go needs all the encouragement he can get, and this one was lucky to have a Dad who ladled it out in great dosages.

1775 Broadway
November 8, 1939

My dear Pal Bill:

We arrived home safely after a most happy weekend with you and Dave.

I was tremendously pleased to see the progress you are making and how you are fitting into the school's activities, in spite of the little difficulties you have experienced with some of your fellow students.

I was glad to hear of your interest in the local school paper and your association with the editor. Keep it up because it is wonderful experience, and will help you to develop leadership, which will be so essential in later years.

Both Mother and I were so pleased with the type of men and women who are in this school and the manner in which they run it. It is a wonderful institution, and one of the most beautiful countrysides I have ever seen with a healthy climate.

Just keep your nose to the wind and your chin up and do not let little things worry you because I know you have got it in you to be up among the leaders in your class in the near future.

With love and best wishes,

As ever,

Daddy

Wm. F. Rickenbacker
The Asheville School
Asheville, North Carolina

1775 Broadway
April 11, 1940

My dear Pal Bill:

As you know one of the most important items in life is to never spend more than you take in or earn, and always save a portion of your earnings for a rainy day or some unexpected misfortune.

In order to fully appreciate this fact, I am sending you a Journal so you can keep a record of the money you receive or have in your personal account at the school and on hand in the one column, and in the other the details of what you spend. Then at the end of each month, you will know exactly where you stand by subtracting the expenditures from the balance or amount received at the first of the month.

This is very important and will be of great value to you in later years, if you start now, so be sure to make a business of keeping a daily record of your expenditures.

Of course you realize how valuable your diary is

covering the wonderful trip we all had last summer, particularly in view of the unfortunate turn of the war which is taking place in many of the harbors and cities where we spent so many happy hours.

It does not seem possible that these fine people—quiet and peace loving—could be in the throes of war, and that the beautiful country and towns we visited are being bombarded by battleships and airplanes. Your diary will become all the more valuable as years go on because it is truly historical.

With love and best wishes,

As ever,

Daddy

Wm. F. Rickenbacker
The Asheville School
Asheville, North Carolina

1775 Broadway
May 17, 1940

My dear Pal Bill:

I am attaching herewith copy of letter to Dave and am curious to know whether he mentioned Mother's Day to you, and if so why you did not wire her.

Mother's birthday is on Monday, May 20, and am sure she would love to have a few words of greeting by telegram from you.

I was out yesterday afternoon on Long Island and played eighteen holes of golf without throwing my back out of joint, but the score was nothing to brag about.

With love.

As ever,

Daddy

William F. Rickenbacker
The Asheville School
Asheville, North Carolina

*With Dad and Sheppy always on hand to stimulate our memory
of birthdays, anniversaries, and other important occasions, it's
a wonder we ever learned to remember anything at all. For years
the standard gesture was a dozen red roses. Sometimes we got
our signals crossed and Mother would receive a dozen red roses
three or four times over—as ordered by Sheppy ("love from Eddie"), Dad ("love from Dave and Bill"), and maybe even Dave
or me. We still love red roses.*

✳   ✳   ✳

10 Rockefeller Plaza
October 21, 1941

My dear Bill:

It was nice to have a chance to talk to you the
other night and to know you are getting along so well
with your studies at school but, very frankly, I was
terribly disappointed and shocked by your last letter as
I know you are entirely too keen and sympathetic to
mean what you said about your brother Dave.

In the first place you must learn not to criticize
and above all your own, for some day it will

17

bounce back on you and hurt many times more.

Instead of criticizing brother Dave, you should be out promoting his welfare. Learn to fight for him as I know he would fight for you in a pinch. He has proven that often.

He may not get along with Latin and algebra as well as you do, but he knows how to make friends and keep them, and that is what I want you to do. Learn to make people like you by being gracious, sympathetic and thinking of their welfare before you think of your own.

You two boys have got to learn to have mutual respect and admiration for each other, bearing in mind that you both will always have opportunities to improve your own welfare in your own way, and that neither of you will ever be perfect.

I know you are qualified to do what I recommend. It is all up to you because, very frankly, if you cannot change your way of thinking, then I am going to have to change it for you, which I do not want to do. In other words, I mean if you cannot learn to love and respect Dave for what he really is, as well as your fellow students, you probably would be much better off in a military school, which is not an easy life and where they teach you these traits by compulsion instead of persuasion. That, I do not want to do, only as a last resort, and I know you will help me to prevent it.

Love and best wishes

As always,

Daddy

William F. Rickenbacker
Asheville School
Asheville, North Carolina

Youngsters will fight, especially if they're brothers. Dad knew that, but he must have remembered his own boyhood when the very survival of his family—a widowed mother and seven children—depended on their clinging together and working for each other. Against that background, a suggestion of brotherly malice was outright heresy. The early traits were genuine, by the way: to this day my brother Dave is a far more likable, friendly, and warmhearted man than I am.

★   ★   ★

Rockefeller Plaza
November 11, 1941

My dear Pal Bill:

Today is Armistice Day for World War No. 1 that
ended twenty-three years ago at eleven o'clock.

It hardly seems possible that we are involved in
another one more deadly, and in spite of conditions we
have got to make the best of everything.

Love, as ever,

Daddy

William F. Rickenbacker
Asheville School
Asheville, North Carolina

Miami, Florida
March 8, 1942

My dear Bill:

I was happy to have the chance to talk to you today by long distance, but sorry I will not have the privilege of being with you during your vacation but we, as a country, are at war and since I can be of some real help to my fellow countrymen, I am going to take advantage of it, in spite of physical deficiency.

Love and best wishes,

As ever,

Daddy

William F. Rickenbacker
Asheville School
Asheville, North Carolina

Dad's contribution to the war effort, referred to here, was his global inspection tours as a personal emissary of the Secretary of War. For a year or two there are very few letters from him.

★　　　★　　　★

10 Rockefeller Plaza
April 24, 1943

My dear Pal Bill:

In all probability you have heard from Mother since she has been in Miami but I talked to her last night on long distance and she seems to be improving fortunately.

Confidentially, I am leaving the country for a period of about six weeks. I am going to North Africa via South America and then on to Egypt, India, China and if it works out as I expect it to, I will come back through Russia to North Africa, then to England, Ireland, Greenland, Labrador, Newfoundland and home. In other words, it is completing my secret missions for Secretary of War Stimson.

I am taking Colonel Bill Nuckols with me and also Dr. Dahl from Atlanta in order to get my bones cracked once or twice a day and keep the circulation moving.

I just finished up a contract for my movie and the writers are on the job putting my life's indiscretions together with the hope that it will be ready for the screen about December 15, 1943.

Have you heard about the story of the two sea gulls who got lost in the Sahara Desert and after about ten days or two weeks, without food or water, they were so famished and burning with thirst that one said to the other "Let's pray," and believe it or not, Rickenbacker came down and landed right on his head —"from the sublime to the ridiculous."

Love and best wishes

As always,

Daddy

William F. Rickenbacker
Asheville School
Asheville, North Carolina

"Getting the bones cracked" was the daily massage Dad needed after the horrible crash in Atlanta in February of 1941. Dad's association with sea gulls was immortalized in October of 1942 when, with six other men, he was downed in the Pacific and survived three weeks of drifting in life rafts—thanks largely to a sea gull that floated down from Heaven one day and landed on Dad's fedora.

★   ★   ★

Edward V. Rickenbacker
New York City

November 3, 1944

My dear Pal Bill:

I am sorry not to have written you sooner, but as usual I have been jammed to the funnels with work.

I noticed what you had to say in your last letter about your experience with the liquor dealer the night of your waffle party.

It is unfortunate that the boy you speak of has so little mental control of himself that he becomes a party to such affairs and with such people.

My only hope is that he will learn the error of his ways soon enough to prevent a mistake which will have to be paid for all the years of his life by himself.

That is one of the reasons that I have always through your life given you the privilege of taking a cocktail or a glass of beer with us at home whenever you wanted it, or with our friends.

This individual freedom, and confidence on my part, I know will never be abused.

Well, the election is just around the corner and what happens on next Tuesday may have a good or bad effect on the future generations of this great country of ours for a long time to come.

I am praying for your generation's sake, and those that follow you, that the American people will realize on November 7 what a glorious country they live in, and what freedoms and standard of living they are enjoying—a heritage no other peoples in the world can boast of.

Unfortunately, there are many, due to selfishness and greed, who are willing to sacrifice the welfare of their nation for a momentary gain for themselves by taking advantage of the ignorance of the masses whom they are trying to convince, and many of them have been convinced, that the world owes them a living without working and fighting for it. That never has been true and never will be true. Your Daddy is a living example of the opportunities and liberties this nation offers. I want them reserved for you as they were for me.

Love and best wishes.

As always,

Daddy

Mr. William F. Rickenbacker
The Asheville School
Asheville, North Carolina

Because of his own father's death, Dad had to leave school before finishing the seventh grade. All of his achievements are profoundly his own, without benefit of formal education. With this in mind, his generosity toward school and schooling is genuinely amazing, and a very good measure of his largeness of soul. The experience with liquor had to do with my tagging along when an older lad purchased some white lightning from a bootlegger down by the railroad tracks. I was scandalized at the time. Actually it was an honorable transaction. Writing to a son now sixteen, Dad begins to give more attention to public affairs and questions of state.

★   ★   ★

Edward V. Rickenbacker
New York City

January 29, 1945

My dear Pal Bill:

Sorry I have not written you sooner since the
Holidays, but I have been out of town almost
constantly.

Naturally, we are enjoying your letters
tremendously and I got a great kick out of your
description of the new boys in the letter you wrote
after you had been back to school for about a week.

Probably they will have the same privilege and
pleasure as the years go on and will look back with a
great deal of amusement at their original years, the
same as you are able to today.

It certainly must be gratifying to be so far ahead in
your Spanish. You must also be getting a great kick out
of your oil painting. It is certainly a grand hobby and
one that you can always use.

I used to have a love for water colors in my school
days, but I was much younger than you are now.
However, keep it up.

During this month I have been out to the Coast to visit the Lockheed people, and also the Douglas plant. At Lockheed I saw the new Constitution mock-up. This is the biggest airplane in this country, carrying one hundred and fifty passengers, with four 3,500 horsepower Pratt & Whitney Major engines. It is a double decker with a winding stair-case from the lower to the upper deck, and has all the comforts of home.

It will carry one hundred and fifty passengers non-stop from New York to London or Paris. Some airplane!

I also had a chance to see the Lockheed new jet propulsion Spider plane and it is a honey. It will do approximately six hundred miles per hour and they are just getting started in production. Of course, this is off the record.

The Douglas DC-7 is approximately a one hundred passenger ship and not quite as large as the Constitution, or as good looking for it is only a single decker. It will go from New York to London or Paris, non-stop. It is still some airplane.

Love and best wishes with a hope of hearing from you soon.

As always,

Daddy

The following is one of the very few handwritten letters I have from Dad. It is dated December 25, 1944. The wish expressed in the last sentence came true, but peace didn't last long.

E A S T E R N   A I R   L I N E S
Incorporated

Eastern Air Lines Building 10 Rockefeller Plaza
New York

December 25, 1944

Dear Pal Bill:

Not knowing what you would like most as an Xmas remembrance I'm enclosing check which you can use as you like and for something which would fit better than what I could think of at this time.

It's grand having you home with us again.

And my wish for you is that the skies will clear of War clouds before the passing of 1945.

As always,

Daddy

Edward V. Rickenbacker
New York City

February 2, 1945

My dear Pal Bill:

We were delighted to hear that you have been in contact with Dartmouth College. In spite of the fact that I never went to college but have a trunk full of degrees, I am sure they will have no alternative but to welcome you.

There are several Dartmouth men in the organization and they cannot speak too highly of the advantages to be gained.

Naturally, if you decide to go to Dartmouth, I shall be happy to cooperate with you and instead of your being forced to quit when you are eighteen, I am sure that the Army Air Forces would be delighted to let you complete the semester.

I am also awaiting the return of Colonel Earle Johnson, who is head of the Air Cadet organization, in order to get the detailed information necessary to

permit you to carry on as a Cadet in the Air Forces
after you become eighteen.

All in all, I feel you will be better off and will be
pleased with the combination of arrangements between
Dartmouth and the Air Forces if they can be worked
out to your satisfaction, which I am sure they can.

Love and best wishes,

Daddy

Mr. William F. Rickenbacker
Asheville School
Asheville, North Carolina

*Dad was extremely eager to have me go to Dartmouth—perhaps
in the hope that fresh air and outdoor sports would counterbal-
ance my intellectual tendencies. As it turned out, Dartmouth
was spared.*

★   ★   ★

Edward V. Rickenbacker
New York City

March 26, 1945

My dear Pal Bill:

To start with, we have had three wonderful letters
—dated March 12, March 16, and March 18,
respectively—without my having had an opportunity to
answer any one of them until today, Sunday a.m., at the
office, and what a beautiful day it is! Just about the
type of day that I could shoot about a 74 at Sleepy
Hollow, at least on the first nine.

Starting with your March 12th letter, I would not
worry too much about what some members of the
faculty think of golf, or of a golf course, for there is no
doubt in my mind, and I am sure you agree, that they
have good reason for thinking that some of the boys do
take advantage of them both in smoking and drinking
and, at the same time, with swank and show, that do
not add to their behavior.

If I were you, I would not take seriously what the

faculty thinks of these cases—at least I would not take them personally—because you surely know they are not true concerning you, and in view of that fact you can well afford to have a free conscience and not harbor any illusions or delusions concerning what they might think of you personally. In other words, do not let things of this sort worry you or get your goat. You are too big mentally.

The letters from Dave come consistently but not frequently enough to satisfy us. I know he has many other problems and cannot be as free and interesting as you can, but it must be remembered that he is in the Army and that there is a strict censorship clamped on anything the boys may have to say, which, of course, is not helping their peace of mind or anyone else's. But that is war.

As for his female advice to you, I would not worry about that either. He probably had a kidding streak on his mind that morning and thought he would give a little old-fashioned advice to his younger brother, because there isn't much doubt in my mind that Dave has learned a lot of things during the past two years that he would not have learned if he had not been in the Army.

I do not know who this new found love of yours is, called "Sandy," but apparently it is something that dates back to the dark ages; however, it does add to your variety of correspondence.

Chapter II

Now comes your second letter of March 16 which was written on your 17th birthday and in a philosophical manner, which we both enjoyed very much.

You have progressed rapidly through the years and there is no question but what your sixteenth year was a fruitful one, and only time will prove how fruitful it was to you, individually, and to millions of others.

I have never worried about your succeeding in anything that you apply yourself to and I am sure that you are convinced of this fact from your own statements.

I am more than happy to hear that you have enlarged your list of new friends and made fast your many old friendships, for, after all, one of the greatest attributes any man can have is to learn to like people in order that they will learn to like him.

This is evidenced more positively with dogs. If a man loves animals it is very simple for them to understand it in their dumb way and soon they reciprocate to the best of their ability by loving you.

I agree with your thinking with reference to politics, particularly on the diplomatic side. There is great need today for straight thinkers and honest actors, and as time goes on these United States of America will need the kind of men that I am sure you are going to develop into, supporting and acting in behalf of this country and its people, not only for the benefit of us alone but for the people of the world as a whole.

Yes, you can be tolerant. You have proven it to us and it is a trait that I know you will want to expand on as time goes on.

Do not worry too much about living on borrowed time and that this will be your last civilian year for at least three or four years more, because I frankly feel, with the way things are going in Europe, that the Germans will collapse completely this summer with the exception of some guerrilla warfare that will take a few months longer to clean up.

And if you have read any of the newspapers recently of the damage we have been doing to the heart of Japan with our navy aircraft and our B-29s, I am not so sure that that is going to last too long either; in fact, I am sure that the Russians will come in on our side at Siberia and that should help shorten the war by years.

In fact, it is fairly possible that since you have a year of civilian life ahead of you and a year of training in one of the services you make up your mind you are going to join, even the Japanese war might be over by that time, with the exception of guerrilla warfare which will be taken care of by the regulars in the

Army and the Navy, for that is their business and life's work as career men in our military services.

Meaning that you will have the benefit of probably a year in the service and learn a lot that will stand you in good stead in the years to come. And the fact that you will break into your college career for one year will, in my opinion, prove very beneficial, for you will have a much broader understanding of life itself and the problems that go with it and, consequently, be more practical in your application to your studies in your remaining college years, which will be based upon practical knowledge and not theory alone.

Your association with new-found friends in your first year of college will be very beneficial and I am sure happy in all respects. As for your association with the boys in whatever branch of the Service you decide to join up with, I am not worried about your making friends with them, or their wanting to make friends with you. You've got it—I mean the "know-how" as well as the desire, which comes from the heart and which they too will have and understand.

Chapter III

Gosh! You certainly get me down with your great, big words. I have to go to the dictionary to look up the meaning of them, to say nothing of your French quotations. You know it has been a long time since I spoke French in World War I, and I have forgotten most of what little I knew.

You know, one of the greatest speakers and writers of our time was President Woodrow Wilson and his theory always was to say what he wanted to say in simple terms and words so that the average man would understand and appreciate what he was trying to tell them. I think that is a good idea too. It saves a lot of headaches.

Yes, it was grand to talk to you on the evening of your birthday. I was only afraid that we might not be able to reach you and I did so want to hear your voice again. So did Mother. You were right. I was sitting there with my slippers on in the old chair consuming a delicious old-fashioned, just finished listening to the 7:15 news, and was getting ready to hear my favorite, the Lone Ranger at 7:30. In the intervening fifteen minutes we were able to talk to you. Then came some of Anne's delicious cookies, the reading of the newspapers and then going to bed, satisfied and happy, with Heine's aroma in my nostrils.

Mother and I were delighted to hear that you have only three or four pages to go of the thirty-two pages of Beethoven's Sonata. Surely this takes application and concentration, of which you can be very proud, and I will be anxious to hear you play Beethoven's Sonata on your return in June.

Personally, I would give my shirt if I could play the piano, because one gets so many, many happy hours of genuine pleasure without having to look to the outside world and the many superficial interests that are of only momentary existence. Keep on studying; keep on playing. It will go well with any profession you choose; in fact, it will multiply whatever you do in value to yourself as well as others.

Love and best wishes, and I am looking forward to seeing you in the not too distant future.

As always,

Daddy

Mr. William Rickenbacker
Asheville School
Asheville, North Carolina

The "Sandy" mentioned had been, ten years earlier, a childhood playmate, and was now a pen pal. Since 1955 she has been my beloved wife. The Beethoven was part of a recital I gave at graduation. My fondness for rare words was ever a bone of contention. Twenty years later, in his autobiography, Dad described me, half-amusedly, as possessing "a vocabulary larger than the English dictionary." In 1945 I was preparing for a career in philology.

★　　　★　　　★

Edward V. Rickenbacker
New York City

April 23, 1945

My dear Pal Bill:

Well a lot of things have happened in the last week or ten days. Of course, the death of the President surprised a lot of people, but not me because I had understood how seriously ill he has been for months past.

Mr. Truman I am sure will make a real President because he knows he doesn't know everything and, therefore, will surround himself, in my opinion, with a lot of good men which is the one outstanding opportunity that any man has when he becomes President of these United States; that is, to commandeer the best brains available. It just goes to show that this country is bigger than any one man or any dozen men, and, in my opinion, it was an act of fate that will level out our future and get us out on an even keel again, because Mr. Truman comes from the soil back in the Middle West where he learned the value of America in his early youth.

The thing that made me learn to admire Mr. Truman was the fact that after he had been criticized and lambasted by the opposing politicians during the elections, for his early association with the Prendergast political gang in Kansas City, he then, after election, attended Mr. Prendergast's funeral in the face of all the opposition and possible criticisms and suggestions not to do it. He did it because of the fact that he had been befriended by Mr. Prendergast in his early years. It showed real guts on Mr. Truman's part which always means character. It is the American way of doing things.

Things are moving very rapidly in Europe, but it is still a very deadly war. As I listened to the radio this morning about how Berlin is being mauled and wiped off the face of the earth, I couldn't help but realize that we are living in a funny old world today. Such carnage as must be taking place in Germany is unbelievable, and then when you see the pictures of the way the atrocities are perpetrated by the Germans on the poor slave laborers, refugees and prisoners of war, I have no sympathy for them or what is happening to them; but it is going to take time to wipe out the fanatics because there are still a lot of strongholds in the mountains that will take a lot of our boys' lives before we finally clean up the show to a complete victory.

I am hoping that when Germany's organized efforts capitulate, maybe Japan might capitulate also within a short period thereafter, but am afraid that is wishful thinking on my part. However, it doesn't do any harm to wish.

Things are going ahead nicely with Eastern Air Lines and, of course, we look forward to a great year, but the headaches are beginning to develop and I am sure will multiply as time goes on, due to the rapid expansion we are making.

Love and best wishes, and am looking forward to seeing you at Commencement time.

As always,

Daddy

Mr. William Rickenbacker
Asheville School
Asheville, North Carolina

Edward V. Rickenbacker
New York City

May 7, 1945

My dear Pal Bill:

Well, here we are again—Mother, Anne and Perry
—all on the Hauser Elimination Diet; in fact, this is the
fifth day and we think we might live.

Yes, in accordance with your last letter there are
forty days more of school, at a school that has done you
a great deal of good, and—to put it the other way, too
—one that you have taken the maximum advantage of
in order to learn as much as possible. Frankly, Mother
and I are very happy with the results.

I am sure, as the years go on, you will look back at
Asheville with a great deal of pleasure and pride, but
then again it doesn't make much difference what
school you go to. It depends upon your desires and
ambitions to learn. Remember Lincoln became
President by going to school before the fire light and
fireplace and from books only, without any tutors.

Mother said she wrote you with reference to the possibility of taking the whole summer off, in view of the conditions and the progress of the war.

Very frankly, I think you should give it some serious thought, because, after all, I am sure that if you started your college career in September you would get the opportunity to finish a complete year before going into the service, if that happens to be necessary at that time, which I am praying to God it won't be.

I am changing my thinking slightly with reference to the Japanese wanting to stick it out until the last Jap is dead. With the rapid collapse of Germany which may be within a day or two, or before you get this letter, with the exception of a few isolated pockets which will not last long; and if Russia goes into Siberia against Japan to protect their own political position in Asia, and if we will double our efforts in the Pacific, aided by whatever the British contribute—the Japs may capitulate completely.

It may be wishful thinking, but that may be the result of the fanaticism and the fanatical minds that exist in Japan. Only such fanaticism can make a complete reversal, but normal thinking people could not be expected to do so and would not do so.

Then again, if there is one man in authority who can get the Japanese to lay down their arms, it is possible that the industrialists, financiers, business people and educators in general might get him on their side instead of the war mongers' side. If so, it is possible that there will be a capitulation or unconditional surrender before it will be necessary for us to carry on and lose many thousands of our American boys and billions' worth of material, to bring about the unconditional surrender on the battlefield.

It is only natural that the clear-thinking Japanese, who are not at the moment in power, would prefer to offer us conditional surrender and save their homes and the material things rather than carry the war on, losing millions of their men plus their homes and factories, and then be forced into unconditional surrender the same as Germany has. Maybe it is wishful thinking. I hope not.

Your comments with reference to Communism and Socialism are so basically sound that it is startling, and yet we must not forget that the world rotates in cycles and, consequently, so do human beings. Many of the professors will, I am sure, awaken to that realization before they go along very much further; and as for the students, they certainly can be forgiven temporarily for their failure to see through the haze and the mist into the clear future.

I had the good fortune to read your editorial in "Ashnoca" and congratulate you on the beautiful manner in which it was written and theme that you picked. It is something you will always be proud of, as we are.

In the meantime, don't wait until V-day. Write us several days before.

Love and best wishes.

As always,

Daddy

Mr. William Rickenbacker
Asheville School
Asheville, North Carolina

Edward V. Rickenbacker
New York City

May 14, 1945

My dear Pal Bill:

We were tickled pink to receive your last letter
and to know that you will not have to start college (at
Harvard) before September and that you will be with
us all summer. It is almost like a dream coming true.

I want you to know that your choice of Harvard
has my 100% approval, as well as Mother's and we
know that you will benefit, in a great measure, by
going there. It makes us both feel proud as punch to
know that we have a boy qualified to the degree that
you have proven yourself to be.

As I wrote you last Sunday, I believed that in all
probability V-E Day would come to pass before you
even received my letter, and now we are all duly
grateful that it has happened and thank God for the
end of the War in Europe. I only wish we could say
the same for the Pacific, but am afraid we have a long,
hard war out there unless the Japanese industrialists
and financial interests get the ear of the Emperor and
overrule the war mongers.

About the simplest way to bring that about is to

bomb hell out of them and burn or blow up their factories and homes, in order to make them realize that we have the upper hand without any serious opposition.

Of course, they have the only big reservoir of fighting man power left on the ground—between four and six million soldiers. On the other hand, they won't do too much good if they haven't factories or airplanes, as well as supplies to keep them going in the field. That is the air job that lies ahead of us.

If Russia comes in, and with our increased pressure and the help of the British, it is possible the Japs might see the light of day and surrender unconditionally in advance of total destruction such as took place in Germany.

I only wish that Dave could be home with us this summer, but that, of course, is impossible and we will have to hope for the best.

You would be interested in seeing the entertainment square down in Rockefeller Center. They have just put in a miniature size aircraft carrier, to scale, which takes up the whole sunken garden. There are planes on the deck and all the details, to scale, even to having simulated the ocean and the waves with canvas properly colored from the water line down.

The Navy designed and built it and it is understood to have cost in the neighborhood of $100,000. The purpose of it is to stimulate the Seventh War Bond Campaign which opens today and carries through for two or three months.

They are charging the public—how much I don't know—to go through its innards and to walk on the deck. I am sure you will get a bang out of taking a look at it because they say it is quite a masterpiece.

I don't know what you plan to study at Harvard, or what you have chosen as your main theme song. However, I would appreciate your giving some thought to having one of your courses Business Administration, because it will stand you in mighty good stead no matter what walk of life you choose or follow. We can discuss that during the summer months at our leisure.

There is no doubt but what the European situation is really going to bring about a lot of headaches insofar as reconditioning the Germans and rehabilitating the conquered lands and peoples is concerned.

It is gratifying to know that Hitler, Mussolini, Goebbels and a dozen or so others of the war mongers saw fit to commit suicide and save the time and energy to destroy them.

I am disappointed in their lack of action in handling Petain, particularly Laval, Goering, Himmler,

Doenitz and many others. They should have been tried within a day or two, or three days, after their capture and sentenced the maximum, which is death, for their criminal activities.

Love and best wishes.

As always,

Daddy

P.S. You forgot Mother's Day? Don't forget Mother's birthday May 20th.

Mr. William Rickenbacker
Asheville School
Asheville, North Carolina

I had been persuaded that Harvard was more suitable for my purposes than Dartmouth, which was not known in 1945 for its department of comparative philology. Dad, though he was severely disappointed, nevertheless gave me full and generous support from this moment forward. It was a good lesson: from now on the one responsible for my decisions was me. He would back me up, but I was on notice that the consequences were to be mine. A wise decision by him, and not a completely bad one by me: I loved Harvard and have always been grateful for my years there.

★   ★   ★

COLLEGE YEARS

★　★　★

1945-1949

Edward V. Rickenbacker
New York City

November 7, 1945

My dear Pal Bill:

We were delighted to receive your nice letter of
Monday after midnight, but I think you ought to go to
bed earlier and get up earlier in the morning because
you know the old saying goes that the sleep before
midnight is more valuable than that after.

Then again, your mind is much clearer early in the
day than any other part of the day.

In my opinion, there is very little constructive
thinking done after three o'clock in the afternoon,
particularly when important decisions are made, and
certainly never make decisions in bed. Reading and
writing in the wee hours of the morning are usually the
best, but not decisions.

It was nice meeting your room mate and in spite
of his caffeine I think he is a rather decent chap. As
time goes on he will get over his prejudices and

semi-communistic ideas, particularly when he has to learn to make his own living.

Do not overdo the swimming—take it gradually and build up to the ultimate. It is much easier on the constitution.

You must have looked that dictionary over very carefully with all the big words you used in your letter. I am sorry I have no time to find the dictionary and get their exact meaning, but I think I catch on.

In your writing of treatises always remember you are honest at heart and have the convictions balanced by common sense. There is no harm in stating your case frankly and sincerely.

It has been my experience that once people find out you believe what you say, even though you are wrong now and then, you are admired for it much more than if you become nothing more than a "yes man" and always take the easy road out.

It was grand being with you and with oceans of love, as Walter Winchell would say, I remain,

Your New York correspondent,

Daddy

Mr. William F. Rickenbacker
Harvard University
Cambridge, Massachusetts

★　　　★　　　★

Edward V. Rickenbacker
New York City

March 18, 1946

My dear Pal Bill:

As you know by now, I made a hurried trip to
California due to Grandmother's serious illness.
Fortunately, she had rallied from what looked like a
case of pneumonia from which the doctors did not
expect a recovery if it carried on.

It is rather pathetic to have one grow so old—one
who has done so much in the world and given so much
to others. She seems to have arrived at the end of her
rope so to speak, being extremely thin and having no

body resistance. She is more or less living on her will power.

Fortunately for me, she was quite rational and had not lost her sense of humor, but there is nothing that can be done for her other than to give her the best medical care and attention which we are doing by having a day and night nurse with her in the hospital and the attention of the best doctors in Los Angeles.

She may live for days, weeks, or months, and it is regrettable because she realizes that she is at the end of her rope and can do nothing about it. As much as I hate to lose her, she would be better off to pass along in her sleep and eliminate the suffering of mental anguish which she must be experiencing as she looks back over a long, arduous life.

I note in your letter a tendency on your part to belittle the so-called exclusive clubs and exclusive people. Remember, it is very easy with your attitude to become the isolationist instead of them, and if you let this attitude multiply, you will soon find yourself a snob instead of the other fellow.

I say this knowing that your judgment is good and that you will be able to balance off all of your interests and not abuse any of them in any way. We must always remember that life has many, many angles and many, many types of people—good, bad, and indifferent. Sometimes those that seem bad today turn out to be the good ones tomorrow and vice versa. Consequently, in our daily dealings with all types, we will have to balance our judgment and be fair and just to all. Otherwise, eventually, we suffer the consequences ourselves.

You ,are doing a grand job at school and all of us are terribly proud of you and your accomplishments, but I do not want you to get into the mood of discrediting individuals or groups simply because it may be the vogue of the day because vogues change very rapidly.

I know you will take these suggestions of mine in the right light because they are the results of a great many years of life and a million contacts with all types of people all over the world.

I hope that your birthday was a happy one and my regrets as well as Mother's that we couldn't be with you to help celebrate it.

But then, I know that there will be many, many more in the future, and I hope that, as years go on, you will expand in stature of mentality as you have in the past for there is need more so today for a well-balanced mentality and energetic and courageous intelligence than ever before in the history of this country or the world at large.

With love and best wishes as always,

Daddy

Mr. William F. Rickenbacker
Harvard University
Cambridge, Massachusetts

★　　★　　★

Edward V. Rickenbacker
New York City

April 21, 1946

My dear Pal Bill:

Today is Easter and what a beautiful day. All of
the gals are on the street with their new bonnets and
finery. Untold thousands are going to church, which is
a wonderful thing because too many of us have gotten
away from the simple things in life and that
fundamental faith in the Power Above, and we have
lost the true beauty of living to a degree.

Too many millions want something for nothing and
are interested only in the superficial things in life—that
goes the world over.

I have noted from your recent letters, particularly one, that you refer to Dean Leighton's calling you in on the carpet. This is not unusual in the life of boys your age, but I am sure you recognize the value of the advice and will heed it and take advantage of all the opportunities that are yours.

I think, as I always have felt, that you should make every effort to learn to have people like you or rather first learn to like people by being sympathetic and interested, and they in turn cannot help but like you. This is vital in your future, and important in whatever path you pursue.

There is no harm in flippant remarks [except] when they are made in the wrong place and at the wrong time, but that is where judgment comes in on your part. You must learn to be loyal to your school because after all there have been a lot of great men graduated from Harvard as a result of the long, long effort on the part of brilliant men who have been masters at the school. Therefore, you should first of all be loyal and understanding, as well as considerate of the privileges they offer.

Surely no one knows better than your good self the value of all of the knowledge available at Harvard, and maybe you must give up some of your social activities to be able to keep up with what no doubt is a trying pace of learning, but you can and will do it.

I am glad to hear that your swimming activities have caused aches but not in your ears. Watch yourself carefully because you will realize as the years go on the value of good hearing and good eyesight. Today, it seems unimportant to a degree. Now is the time to protect them for the future.

I do not know what is going to happen to the draft situation, but I hope that it works out all right so be philosophical about it. Do not let it get you upset emotionally or cause you to worry because if you use the same philosophy that I have—what is to be will be —there isn't much you can do about it but take it, like it, and make the best of it, as you will be much happier and so will those around you. This I am sure you can do.

Further, I am certain that your marks will improve as time goes on, and I wish you would make a business of showing your appreciation of the professors, and particularly Dean Leighton's recommendations and advice. In fact, make a business of getting acquainted with him and discussing your problems in order that he may help you to recognize your hopes and wishes.

I would investigate what the Navy is doing with reference to their military and air corps activities. Get the lowdown on it and let me have the results from your investigation. Also check with the young lady who seems to know all about the draft and get the benefit of her recommendations and pass them on.

Hans Adamson showed me a letter with reference to his biography of myself, and I hasten to compliment you on the beautiful tribute you paid to me. It is worthy and compensates me in a great measure for the years I have had with you.

I am planning to get out a special edition and dedicate it to the members of the Eastern Air Lines Family in order that they too may know the ups and downs of my life and the type of leadership that they are following and be guided accordingly.

This has been rather a rambling letter, but I know you understand it. Also, I know that you are qualified to get into the groove and stay there for your own benefit and the benefit of friends which you wish to make and hold for the balance of your life.

With love and best wishes.

As always,

Daddy

Mr. William F. Rickenbacker
Harvard University
Cambridge, Massachusetts

Here I was, criticizing a college I had insisted on going to against his wishes. The temptation must have been strong for him to remind me of that—but Dad was too big to stoop for little games. As a matter of fact, I kicked up my heels and managed to get on probation.

★   ★   ★

Edward V. Rickenbacker
New York City

May 20, 1946

My dear Pal Bill:

It was grand having the privilege of talking to you on the telephone, if only for a few minutes, the other night in Boston during the few hours that I was there to dedicate our new hangar and take care of the brass hats that were there to do us honor.

I found your three-page letter that you had mentioned, and I am delighted at its contents. Your general progress and the progress you are making with the golf team are grand.

I am particularly pleased with the last paragraph of your letter, and I can assure you that nothing has given me greater satisfaction than to make it possible for you and our pal Dave to get the benefits out of life in your school years that are so essential for the balance of your life in general.

The money that I am spending towards your education gives me more satisfaction than you will ever know, and I am happy that you and Dave have helped throughout the years to inspire me to make the money that makes this education possible.

Consequently, I hope that you will pass up the opportunity to earn $1,500 as a golf pro at the club you have mentioned because I do not think that you would be happy in the first place and in the second place, the years are slipping by, and this summer would be one of the happy ones to have you with us because it would be the first time that the four of us have had the privilege of spending the summer together for several years.

Your position and thoughts are admirable, and I am grateful for your frankness of expression, but see it in our light, and realize that the amount of money that I have spent or expect to spend for your future benefits is a privilege that I shall always cherish.

Because you and Dave are the type of boys who will get the most out of the efforts and the expenditures, which is what I am interested in, I want you both to be prepared by knowledge gained now to be able to place yourselves in a position of being able to earn enough to send your children through school in the years to come.

Consequently, I hope that you will pass up this lucrative opportunity and spend the summer with us where you can enjoy all of the golf that you care to and at the same time have leisure time for studies in preparation for your future.

I am attaching herewith a check for $250, which you may use as in the past, dictated by your own good judgment, for you have been extremely careful with your money, and I know I shall have no quarrel to pick with you ever in this regard.

Love and best wishes.

As always,

Daddy

Mr. William F. Rickenbacker
Harvard University
Cambridge, Massachusetts

Edward V. Rickenbacker
10 Rockefeller Plaza
New York 20

Christmas, 1946

My dear Pal Bill:

With Christmas and the Holiday Season just
around the corner, I am again happy to contribute to
what I hope will become part of your future welfare.
Consequently, I have purchased $3,000 of Government
Series "E" bonds, which in turn will accumulate in
value over the period of the next ten years to the
extent of $4,000, providing they are kept intact.

You are now having the advantage of learning the
benefit of the American way of life, as well as what
opportunities it offers and can do for a young man who
is willing to learn, work, and is always prepared to
coordinate his hands and his head, with the full
realization that one never gets anything for nothing
very long.

The fruits of one's willingness to work and learn in
this land of ours are unlimited—always providing he

keeps his feet on the ground and thinks in terms of fundamentals and is never influenced by the easy way around, or glib promises of horizons without effort.

In building up a nest egg for your future, it is with the realization that you will never forget the old adage "that you can't spend more than you earn, or even as much as you earn and have anything left for a rainy day," is as good today as it was a thousand years ago.

Therefore, always remember never delve into your capital but always save a little out of what you make, for only in that manner can you hope to accumulate. The exception should be only prolonged sickness or extreme emergencies. Full appreciation of the value of the dollar is in your ability and willingness always to want to earn lots.

Make a habit and a promise to yourself that, throughout life after you have finished your schooling, if you haven't earned sufficient money to buy the things you want, do without them until you do have it.

In addition, never buy on time or mortgage your future through time payment plans. If you can't pay cash for that which you want, make a business of doing without it until you can.

This means, regardless of whether your earning power is large or small, always cut your living costs to fit your ability to pay.

As I have asked Mother to put the original of this letter in the safety deposit box with the Government bonds for you, is the reason for your receiving just a copy.

Love and best wishes.

As always,

Daddy

Mr. William F. Rickenbacker
New York City

Edward V. Rickenbacker
10 Rockefeller Plaza
New York 20

January 26, 1947

My dear Pal Bill:

Well, I finally got home, and, as usual, I am taking
advantage of Sunday to clean up the accumulation of
correspondence and problems.

I had been in Washington up until Friday night
due to the Congressional investigation of air accidents,
all of which is time-consuming and most of it palaver.

Unfortunately, the newspaper fraternity, the
railroads, the steamship people, and the ironic critics
who get paid for putting words together have lumped
all of the accidents that took place from one end of the
world to the other, including those in China, India,
England, military, private, charter and contract carrier
accidents, and we, the air transport industry, have
been given credit indirectly for all of them.

And just at this minute, Beverly Griffith called me

and stated that a Dutch airliner crashed at Copenhagen, the airport from which we left while over there, killing nineteen, including the American singer, Grace Moore, and Prince Gustaf of Sweden.

This, of course, will make new headlines by the hour for a few days and radio flashes every hour on the hour—all of which will cause an awful lot of people to quit traveling by air as a great number already have done, as is evidenced by the low load factor, and in general multiply our headaches.

Our accident at Galax, Virginia, was caused by the radio beam at Winston-Salem having gone out at the wrong time, and when it disappeared, the pilot, not knowing the beam was out, ran across the radio beam from Paterson, New Jersey, which is on the same frequency and whose call letters are practically the same. Consequently, he was off course and in coming in on that beam, he crashed into the mountains.

While in Washington, Secretary of War Patterson presented me with a Medal of Merit that is the highest award that can be made to a civilian in accordance with the copy of the citation which is attached.

In other words, I have another to add to the collection.

Generally speaking, business has been terrible in the air transport industry. Many of the companies are in bad financial condition and growing worse and the list is growing longer.

As for our own business, the weather, accidents, and publicity have cut our load factor tremendously and our operating performance is the lowest in the history of the company to date for the month of January.

To give you a better idea of what this month has done to us, we had a Four Million Dollar passenger revenue in the month of December and expanded our organization and spent money in preparation for the increased volume of business to come in January, with the hope and expectation of a Five Million Dollar passenger revenue month which would be necessary over December in order to take care of the additional costs and expenses.

However, to date, we are approximately a million dollars behind December in passenger revenue and instead of a Five Million Dollar Passenger revenue month, we will be lucky to get a Three Million Dollar passenger revenue month, meaning a loss of Two Million Dollars in passenger revenue in one month's time. This also means that it will be the first January that the company will be in red ink since January, 1936.

Conditions in general are not good and are going to get worse as I have anticipated.

Just what is going to happen to a lot of the air transport companies in our industry who are in such bad financial condition is hard to say.

Fortunately for us, the old adage is working again —by saving our cash through the years and keeping our costs down and not spending as much as we make, we are able to weather the storm without being drastically hurt, providing we can keep control of the situation during this trying period for the next year or two which, in all probability, will leave us in the position of being the only one who has been able to weather it.

I hope it was not too much trouble to get back to studying in a serious manner after the Florida fishing and sunshine and that you are both on your way to better and bigger marks in all of your studies.

Love and best wishes.

As always,

Daddy

Mr. William F. Rickenbacker
Harvard University
Cambridge, Massachusetts

CITATION TO ACCOMPANY THE AWARD OF
THE MEDAL FOR MERIT
TO
EDWARD VERNON RICKENBACKER

EDWARD VERNON RICKENBACKER, for exceptionally meritorious conduct in the performance of outstanding services to the United States from December, 1941 to December, 1944. Mr. Rickenbacker, as Special Representative of the Secretary of War and Commanding General, Army Air Forces, made numerous tours of inspection of air bases and air units in theaters of operations throughout the world, and brought to the Air Command plans and recommendations based on his observations that contributed substantially to the fund of knowledge which ultimately brought about the defeat of the enemy. He directed the full facilities of Eastern Air Lines, Inc., of which he was president, to the prosecution of the war, and made available to the Command its air knowledge and experience as well as its operational facilities. Mr. Rickenbacker's great courage and fortitude in the face of the most harrowing physical experiences, and the unflagging zeal and devotion to the cause of his country which he displayed throughout the entire period of hostilities mark him as pre-eminent in the roster of those who rose to their Nation's defense, reflecting the greatest credit on him and the Government and people of the United States.

THE WHITE HOUSE
December 18, 1946.

Edward V. Rickenbacker
10 Rockefeller Plaza
New York 20

Sunday, March 9, 1947

My dear Pal Bill:

Pardon my skipping my Sunday letter to you last week, but we have had one terrific time—at least I have—since a week ago last Friday.

Your report for November, 1946, through January, 1947, arrived last night at home, and, very frankly, Pal, I have no particular qualms to pick with you about your gradings. However, I was terribly shocked to note a copy of the letter dated March 6 from Thomas Mathers, Assistant Dean, to you, attached to the report, covering your probation status and the continuation of it due to your cutting classes while on probation.

Bill, you are a bright boy, but do not forget that you are still a boy. Although you are bright, you are a long way from having balanced judgment and good common sense, which comes through experience and an understanding of human nature plus a desire to want to do the right thing. Do not forget that to want to do the right thing is the most important thing because if you want to, you will find a way.

Please do not feel that you know it all, because if you live to be a million, you will find out that you do not. I do not want you to have to learn the hard way as has been my experience.

Do not let youthful influences surrounding you get the best of you or your judgment, and do not let your prejudices and likes or dislikes for the instructors and professors ruin your common sense or judgment.

You are there to learn, and they are there to teach you. I would abide by their judgment and, certainly, above all, by the rules of the school. Otherwise, the penalty might be so severe that you will regret it all your life—particularly after you grow older and have sense enough to look back and recognize your mistakes and your failure to appreciate advice from elders.

I would appreciate your writing me just what classes you have been cutting and why. In other words, give me the whole story as you honestly see it without any attempt to alibi yourself. Just lay the cards out on the table as I have always tried to teach you, and remember, it is by far the best way at all times.

Then, I would appreciate your going to Dean Mathers, and also to any other Deans that are involved in your welfare and have a heart to heart talk with them. Be frank, honest, and sincere in your apologies for your failures, because this hurts me beyond imagination for I know you know better.

Clean up this probation during the next period in a manner that will be complimentary to you and your good judgment and show your sincerity in wanting to do so.

On Wednesday morning, I am leaving for Mexico City, with the hope of getting the Mexican Government to permit us to extend our services from New Orleans to Mexico City and will not be back until probably next Sunday.

I am looking forward with a great deal of pleasure, hope, and anticipation to your being home with Dave during your Easter vacations and having the opportunity of spending some time with you both.

Love and best wishes.

As always,

Daddy

Mr. William Rickenbacker
Harvard University
Cambridge, Massachusetts

The questioning collegian, trying his hand at all manner of modish hypotheses, runs up against Old Man Common Sense.

★ ★ ★

Edward V. Rickenbacker
10 Rockefeller Plaza
New York 20

November 21, 1947

My dear Pal Bill:

Pardon me for not answering your last letter
sooner, but after reading it, I wondered just how it was
possible to answer it because there are so many
crisscrossings of attitude and questions of conditions, as
well as yourself, that I came to the conclusion that the
simplest way was to ask you just to remember the
simple fundamentals of life when you study and do a
lot of reading. If you can always come back to the
fundamentals or keep them in mind, then you will not
be worried or influenced beyond common sense and
good judgment.

Mother and I suddenly decided to drive up to see
Dave last Saturday. We had a nice ride up and a good
ride back. It is fortunate that we did go because I
doubt that the weather will permit such a trip later.

We found Dave in good spirits and, apparently, doing a good job in his studies—not the best, but a long way from the worst.

It is a beautiful school, but, unfortunately, we did not get to meet the President or any of the faculty because they were all down in Schenectady with the football team and, unfortunately, got licked.

I must report that I did not find the four boys up to snuff in their dormitory because their suite looked like a gypsy pen, and I could not help but spur Dave with the hope that he would clean his own mess up and have the other boys do the same.

Love and best wishes.

As always,

Daddy

Mr. William Rickenbacker
Harvard University
Cambridge, Massachusetts

Edward V. Rickenbacker
10 Rockefeller Plaza
New York 20

Christmas, 1947

My dear Pal Bill:

With Christmas approaching and the opportunity
of having you boys with us over your holiday vacation,
I have been wondering again about an appropriate
Christmas present.

Thinking in terms of long-range rather than
immediate advantages, which I always prefer to do, I
have come to the conclusion again that this Country's
bonds are about as substantial an investment as is
possible to make at any time.

Therefore, I am putting in the safety deposit box
to your credit $3,000 worth of U. S. Government Bonds
which will appreciate to $4,000 in a period of ten
years, with the hope that you will realize you have a
stake in this Nation's welfare.

By having a stake in its welfare, you should, and I
am certain you will, always think in terms of

fundamentals in a realistic and practical fashion, meaning that in addition to your heritage of citizenship which can be excelled by none anywhere in the world and for which you are blessed, you also have a financial stake in seeing that America continues as the land of opportunity and liberty.

No matter what you may learn in college or whatever philosophies you may read about, always remember that the philosophies and the thinking of the creators of this land were realistic and practical first, and, secondly, they were thinking in terms of what they hoped for all generations to come by creating the Constitution and the Bill of Rights, with which we are all fortunate to have been born.

Therefore, let no one influence your better judgment or ever get you off the straight and narrow path in your thinking as well as actions, which, in turn, would destroy the very liberties for which man has fought for centuries.

Unrealistic, impractical thinking, plus selfishness and greed, have brought about totalitarianism and with it enslavement of the masses in most countries throughout the world, to the degree that none can boast of the liberties and standard of living that we can.

If these basic facts are always remembered by you and you are willing to fight for them, your children and their children will enjoy the same privileges that you are enjoying today.

Love and best wishes.

As always,

Daddy

Mr. William Rickenbacker
New York, New York

Edward V. Rickenbacker
10 Rockefeller Plaza
New York 20

February 6, 1948

My dear Pal Bill:

Your letter of February 3 was a real inspiration to read, and I want you to know how happy I am for your two A's and the wonderful compliment of Professor Miller on your essay, which you wrote during your vacation with us in Florida.

Also, I am happy that you listened to his advice with reference to your witty approach to essays, and I am sure that you will benefit accordingly.

How can I refuse to send along a check to one who always dangles the sugar and the honey in the first few paragraphs of his communication?

Consequently, I am attaching my check for $500.00 which will not only take care of your immediate needs but, in a great measure, take care of the problems a couple of months hence—meaning that the next blow will not be as deadly as it would be if I took care of the immediate needs only now.

It does not seem fair for you to criticize my fabulous catches in the Caribbean on the Florida Keys. When two people can catch 110 fish in a few hours, never mind the size—I still think it's miraculous.

Hugh Knowlton's catch was the miracle of the age. As Mother, no doubt, wrote you, he put out a ballyhoo for bait. He caught a three or four pound yellow tail, which, in turn, was caught by about an eighty pound amber jack, which, in turn, was caught by a shark large enough to take all the amber jack from the gills back, leaving Hugh only a nineteen pound head to show for his hour's strenuous effort. Some fish————head!

Love and best wishes.

As always,

Daddy

Mr. William Rickenbacker
Harvard University
Cambridge, Massachusetts

"Professor Miller" was the late Perry Miller. My friends and I took all the courses of his we could wangle our way into. Such men as he are ever the glory of Harvard.

★　　　★　　　★

Edward V. Rickenbacker
10 Rockefeller Plaza
New York 20

February 7, 1948

My dear Pal Bill:

Under separate cover, I am sending you and Dave a copy of "World Communism Today" by Martin Ebon. I know that you are loaded down with a heavy schedule of "must" reading, but, in my opinion, nothing can be more "must" than a clear-eyed view of Communism as it exists today—the causes which make this social cancer grow and the cures that may destroy it.

While it is quite obvious that Martin Ebon is considerably left of center, it is equally clear that he is neither an alarmist nor an apologist when it comes to Communists or Russia.

As you know, there is in the world today a vast amount of hysteria with respect to Communism, and knowing my way of thinking as you do, I need not tell you that, in my opinion, one way to reduce this hysteria is to slap it in the face with facts to strip Communism of the over-earthly mystery in which it has systematically shrouded itself.

"World Communism Today" is well fitted for that purpose. Ebon lays bare the traces of the cancerous, Communistic vein throughout mankind's international anatomy as clearly as a surgeon using his scalpel.

On top of that, his book is not only readable and interesting but, obviously, to a great degree, accurate.

This book is a piece of objective reporting, as I see it, on history in the making.

Love and best wishes.

As always,

Daddy

Mr. William Rickenbacker
Harvard University
Cambridge, Massachusetts

The Ebon book stands up well today.

★ ★ ★

Edward V. Rickenbacker
10 Rockefeller Plaza
New York 20

February 8, 1948

My dear Pal Bill:

Here I am at the office Sunday a.m. after a very hectic Saturday afternoon and evening, caused by what might have been the greatest air transport disaster in the history of air transportation. Fortunately, however, it was not, and I thank God in Heaven for His help in making it possible for the crew to get back to Mother Earth with their cargo of sixty-three passengers. One of the six crew members, unfortunately, was killed when a propeller blade let go on the right hand inboard motor and went through the galley, killing the Flight Steward instantly.

This has certainly been a hectic winter, and I hope that our troubles are over for a long time to come. Fortunately, your old pal, Dick Merrill, was on board as a check pilot and lent a hand in the crisis after the blade let go. No doubt you have read the details of the story of the near accident in the newspapers so I shall not elaborate on it.

Ironically, I was at the University Club, speaking before about three hundred men on the subject of aviation and had just closed my remarks and asked for questions when Hugh Knowlton stepped up and stated that the meeting would have to be closed because I had a very important telephone call. This meant trouble, but I didn't realize how serious the possibilities were until I got the message from the office that one of our New-Type Constellations had developed serious engine trouble about 130 miles off the coast of Jacksonville, Florida, while flying at around 20,000 feet and that they were preparing to "ditch" the ship.

Naturally, I couldn't believe that they could get down from that altitude, if they were on fire, without resulting in a deadly crash to all, and, of course, the rumors were flying right and left about what was happening until, finally, to our great relief, we heard the ship was down at Bunnell, Florida, and that all were safe with the exception of the Flight Steward, who was hit by the propeller blade.

The regrettable part is that there is no evidence left or available to enable us to find out exactly what happened, because when the one blade let go, the unbalanced portion of the other two tore the reduction gear and the front of the engine out and disappeared into the ocean below, as did the broken blade since it kept on going, after killing the Flight Steward, through the other side of the fuselage and out into space.

However, I am grateful for the sake of all that it wasn't as serious as it seemed to be at first.

Now for your letter of January 14, which we received on the boat and which I have held and read several times because I wished to answer it after I had thought it through in order to be absolutely frank and fair to you.

Well do I remember your review of some of the events of your younger years, particularly at Bronxville, which, to me, were some of the happiest years of my life because of the fun I had with you and David in watching you grow physically and mentally.

Surely, Bill, I shall not try to change your hopes and ambitions for a long and useful life, for my one ambition for both you and Dave was to first help you get a sound physical foundation to weather the ruggedness of a long lifetime and, secondly, to be able to give you the best in an education that would expand and balance your mentality to the point where you would learn and be able to serve at the same time and be able to support yourselves and a family in competition with your fellow men during your existence.

My further hope was that you would, in addition

to your own immediate desires, learn a profession that would always be on the shelf in reserve in case you needed it if your own plans did not work out financially or if, in later years, you had a change of heart and mind and would rather do something else.

That is why I had hoped you would take up the law course and do your characteristically good job of learning it at Harvard after you finish your four years of college.

Surely, a good legal training has never hurt or impaired a creative mind but, in most cases, has stimulated it.

I often go back to the thoughts I have had over the years of a diplomatic career or your becoming a career man in our diplomatic corps, which your generation and this country will need very badly.

The legal training would be of great value to you. To get into our diplomatic corps would also give you many advantages in knowing the peoples of the world and their problems, and because of your love of languages and desire to serve, you would be constantly accumulating a fund of knowledge that should further stimulate your creative ability and desires.

All of this would help you along with your present

ambitions if they continue to remain the same because many of our great authors and men of service to mankind have been great lawyers and outstanding diplomats—all of which you can be and still enjoy writing but with a much finer and better foundation and a broader overall knowledge of life, the world, and its people from which to draw your conclusions.

It is my hope and Mother's hope that we can leave you boys substantially protected financially so that such a career would not be impeded for the lack of financial resources in your early years of life while you were growing and raising a family.

So much for your education, ambitions, and hopes.

Now for your statement that you think there is no God or Supreme Being or Power and that anything that has a religious origin may just as easily be derived from pragmatic, practical thinking and, further, that confidence and faith in the Power Above is useless.

Frankly, Bill, only life and its many experiences—good and bad—will bring you to the conclusion sooner or later that there is a God in Heaven.

My own life and experiences should be ample evidence that there is a Supreme Being, because with all the things I have gone through, I must confess it wasn't my knowledge or intelligence that brought me through. It was my faith in God that my life's work had not been completed and that I wanted to continue to live in order to render the maximum service in keeping with my knowledge and ability.

The experience in Atlanta, the Pacific experience, and dozens of other examples have convinced and proved to me that without the Power Above, I wouldn't be here, and without my faith in that Power, my life would have been more or less meaningless and useless.

Our experience yesterday with the Constellation is further evidence of that Power, because from all practical knowledge, and knowing mechanics, the boys should have lost control of the ship which would have crashed at sea with a total of sixty-nine human beings on board.

They were all saved but one, and, surely, they must have been saved for good reasons and the realization that their work was not yet completed.

On the raft in the Pacific, we had two men on board who were atheists—Lt. Whittaker and Col. Adamson. Neither one of them believed in God; in fact, Whittaker had never been in a church or chapel or listened to a sermon until we arrived at the hospital in the Samoa Islands where they had a small chapel and I took him to his first sermon at his request because of what he saw transpire before his very eyes during those twenty-three hectic days and nights.

Since his return to this country, he has given a great amount of his time to the service of God.

And I shall never forget the letter—and I have the original—from Colonel Adamson after I had brought him home and placed him in Walter Reed Hospital in which he stated "not only did you save a man, but you saved a lost soul." Some day, I want you to read the original.

Take your own life and ours. Surely, there was a Power Above that brought us together and thus made possible a happier and fuller life for Mother and myself, and, we hope, a happy, pleasant, comfortable, long and useful life for you.

I know you will read and re-read this letter and take it seriously—as seriously as I have taken the contents of yours—with the hope that both of us shall profit by an expanded mentality and a better understanding of the truth about life itself and the value of service to mankind.

Now I have to dash over to the NBC building for a couple minutes' tribute on the radio—the American Broadcasting Chain—with Mr. Noble, its President, in honor of the achievements and service that Orville Wright rendered this land of ours, its people, and mankind in general by the creation of the airplane.

Love and best wishes.

As always,

Daddy

Mr. William Rickenbacker
Harvard University
Cambridge, Massachusetts

A beautiful reply—far more than my temporary aberration demanded or deserved. "Take your own life and ours." The paragraph that starts with that sentence is the only reference I know of where Dad speaks of having adopted his children.

★　　　★　　　★

Edward V. Rickenbacker
10 Rockefeller Plaza
New York 20

March 17,1948
(Dictated March 14, 1948)

My dear Pal Bill:

Upon my return from California Friday night, I found yours of March 4 and also March 10, and I will try to answer your queries chronologically, as well as tell you what I did and saw while in California. You can guess it—this is Sunday morning, and I am in the office trying to clean up the accumulation on my desk due to my absence of about ten days.

I note from your balance sheet for February that you are Two Dollars in the red, meaning, in all probability, that you have had to do a little borrowing on the side in the interim, which I regret. However, I am sure you will take care of this immediately as I am attaching my check for Two Hundred Dollars, which I hope will carry you through most of the balance of the season, with discretion on your part.

Yes, I can appreciate the importance of making loans to your roommates but with constant vigilance on your part and keeping such loans within the academic family.

Frankly, as I have written you before, I think we're going to be all right in getting the house in Scarborough again, and I am convinced that you will have work enough with all of your studies, the thesis you will be working on, and learning how to speak, write, and understand Russian, as well as trying to get the necessary recreation to keep yourself in good shape physically and mentally.

As for having lost Dave's correct address, that's a poor alibi for having failed to write him. Surely, common sense should dictate that a letter addressed to him at Hamilton College, Clinton, New York, would reach him all right, so don't kid me any more. I am sure he will enjoy receiving that letter which you had tied up in your mind for so long.

I'm glad you saw the picture in the Times, covering my speech to the Protestant Fund organization, and I'm sure that your analysis of the speech is correct because there is a lot of stupid atheism in most schools and colleges, particularly Harvard.

Naturally, I am delighted, and I will be happy to receive your thinking on Christianity and religion, and your assurance that it will be far removed from atheism is consoling, to say the least.

Now, for your letter of March 4. I note that you received my letter the next day, and I'm glad that you noticed there was humor, as well as advice, always coming from Mother and Dad.

You state that the coming summer will be the last four months which you will be able to devote entirely to worthy pursuits. Very frankly, with your background and learning, I think every month for the balance of your life will be devoted to worthy pursuits to fit you, as you say, to be a citizen of this land and a citizen of the world, with high ideals which, through the years, will become clearer, more fundamental, and more

94

practical to you and more beneficial to your generation.

I agree with your next statement that as you learn more, you write simpler, better, and clearer letters. That's why I made the statement above. You also grow calmer and more balanced in your judgment, leaving behind the "boy show-off" manner which always goes with youth.

Yes, I concur that anyone who loses his temper, frankly, loses himself, but at the same time develop and never lose a real sense of humor. It will always stand you in good stead, and you will always be able to see the funny side of even the most serious picture.

As for using Dave's room and being influenced by the beauty of nature and God's gifts from the window, I cannot help but concur with you, but here is where the ability to concentrate comes in, instead of succumbing often to the worldly temptations.

Golf dates and tournament dates would be a wonderful diversion and form of relaxation, and as long as you do not lose your temper and smash a few clubs, I am sure you will qualify.

Yes, I know that you work hard at golf. You work hard at everything you do, but losing weight on a golf course in the summertime, with the exercise, fresh air, and wholesome food that go with it, is an asset at your age instead of a liability. Certainly, no boy of your age has any reason for growing fat at any time until he is too feeble to get around and work it off or too bloomin' lazy to do so.

With reference to the piano, I concur. It is a beautiful piece of machinery and I glory in the pleasure you get out of it. Nevertheless, this, too, can be overdone. On the other hand, there is no one who wants more than I do to see you keep up your music for your own consolation and peace of mind.

Therefore, I have no intention, nor were my above comments and explanations made with any such thought in mind, of knocking down your bowling pins. These are merely details to help balance your thinking.

I have discussed this with Mother again, and we have agreed that the ideal combination for balanced health, a balanced diet, and balanced intellectual, as well as expense, program would be for you to come into the city with me on Monday mornings, do your studying on Mondays and Tuesdays, and your researching at the library. This would give me the opportunity and pleasure of having breakfast with you in the morning and dinner in the evenings when you are free.

Then, you can go back to the country on Wednesday morning, with your head crammed full of learning and your heart full of music, balanced with some good golf on the side.

You would have plenty of room in the apartment for your index references, cataloguing, bibliographies, and all the additional baggage to go along with your researching.

In other words, you will have ample facilities and opportunities to take care of your intellectual and musical cravings while in the city and then have the opportunity of getting the benefits of Nature's and God's gifts while you are in the country. This looks like a sensible program to me.

I agree with you. With the international events which are taking place and the cruel war that Russia is waging on the small countries, a knowledge of the Russian language and the ability to speak it will stand you in good stead, or anyone else, in the years to come.

Frankly, I do not like the trend of things, and I am hoping that the Russian people will awaken to the realization of how close their leaders are driving them to the brink of the canyon before it is too late.

With regard to the Kiplinger letter, I think you misunderstand the reasons for it. It is written not to give you positive conclusions but to report what the Kiplinger people see, hear, and find in their solicitation of viewpoints. This is given to you, and you, in turn, must have the mentality to balance them out and try to form reasonable conclusions for your own benefit and that of others.

The same thing goes for reading the newspapers. Surely, the Palestine, Italian, Chinese, English, the Scandinavian situations, and the rebuilding of Germany are in a sad mess, and tremendous gambles are being taken—they must be under these circumstances—with the hope of preventing more bloodshed on the part of all peoples.

Yes, I concur with you. Selfishness and greed have taken the place of knowledge, idealism, and character —to say nothing of discipline—but maybe it's not as bad as it looks. However, in being able to read the Kiplingers and the newspapers, you are able to have a greater spread of knowledge and, therefore, a better balanced judgment.

I agree with you that the basis of this anti-MacArthur campaign is silly and stupid, but then there are a lot of silly, stupid people in the world because MacArthur is the only statesman who has come out of World War II and is the only man in the world today whom the Russians respect. Therefore, if he did become President, that very respect would postpone, and possibly eliminate, war between Russia and the Western Powers.

His tremendous success, in spite of all the

opposition on the part of ex-President Roosevelt and the brass hats in the Navy and the Army, will stand as a beacon or a lighthouse for future soldiers and statesmen in combat, because, in my opinion, no man can accomplish—and I didn't think even he could—what he did in the Pacific campaign against such tremendous odds and then take Japan without bloodshed or loss of a single life.

If it hadn't been for his statesmanship and great strategy, maybe there would be one or two million less G.I.s to crab about his anti-Democratic and autocratic ways.

Furthermore, most of the G.I. critics never were in the Pacific, and less than one-half of one percent that were there ever came in contact with MacArthur, but they never stop to realize that but for the grace of God and MacArthur, they would not be here today.

I think the subject for your thesis is a good one and will prove of inestimable value to you through the research necessary, to say nothing, of course, of the happiness and pleasure I will get in having you with me on Mondays and Tuesdays when we can discuss the things you are learning, as well as the things I am learning daily.

While in California, I made a deal with Douglas to overhaul our eighteen DC-4's in preparation for next winter, and what a job it is to negotiate a deal of that kind involving so much money when the philosophies existing today dominate. However, it was done and in our favor.

While discussing the DC-9 with Douglas, I think I convinced him that it would be a waste of time to start at this late date to build a plane with reciprocating engines because it would not be ready for three years, and by that time, the progress of jet propulsion engines will be so great that no one would buy the reciprocating engined plane.

Therefore, I pointed out, why not start today to build the same general type planes with jet propulsion and have them ready in four or five years, thereby having something that all air lines would want to buy because they would be up to date. Don't you think that makes sense in view of the fact that the Army, Navy, and all research and experimental workers in the industry are trying to prove the jet engine and have forgotten the reciprocating engine?

For your information, we had been thinking for months in terms of making a movie in technicolor, covering air transportation from the Wrights to rockets, and a grand script was developed by California writers and Hans Adamson, and on arrival in California, they convinced me I should play several of the scenes, which I did trembling with fear.

However, to their surprise as well as my own, I proved to be even better than John Barrymore, and shocking as it may seem—it was to me—I had a make-up man fix me up with the usual cosmetics because of the technicolor demands.

It's going to be a grand picture, but all through it, Eastern Air Lines is woven like a corkscrew, including the New-Type Constellation, in spite of the fact that they talk about everything else in the industry, making it good for the manufacturers, the air transport industry, the military end, and the public as a whole— particularly at this time when air power is so essential.

I know you will get a great kick out of this picture —particularly out of my part—because I thought I had seen and done everything and been everywhere. Now I have added another experience—I'm an actor, movie actor at that.

I think it is a grand opportunity for you to go south this spring to play golf with three or four members of your team, and I am glad they are the older and more responsible element.

Surely, no one knows the penalty of foolish or careless driving more than you, and I hope that you will always assert yourself in the right way. First, never do any driving after you have had any cocktails, and, second, never drive or ride with someone who has, because driving an automobile while under the influence of liquor is like turning loose a crazy man with a couple of six shooters down Broadway or Fifth Avenue during the rush hour and even more hazardous with an automobile because at times the drivers kill themselves as well.

Of course, we'll miss you, but we will know that you are having a good time and benefiting from the experience. Again, it is an opportunity to broaden your perspective and balance your judgment and have fun doing so at the same time.

Love and best wishes.

As always,

Daddy

Mr. William Rickenbacker
Harvard University
Cambridge, Massachusetts

Edward V. Rickenbacker
10 Rockefeller Plaza
New York 20

May 18, 1948
(Dict. May 16)

My dear Pal Bill:

It was grand having you with us on Mother's Day, and Mother enjoyed it more than you will ever know because the kind thought expressed by your presence plus the lovely roses made her very happy.

Now for your letter of April 27 with reference to your attitude and understanding of religion.

In the first place, I can't agree with you that there have been no useful prophets or leaders in religion. Jesus Christ's own record is the greatest of them all.

Secondly, I think that you are to a great degree right in that only through suffering does one get the true and broader concept of religion. However, that is a point which I am trying to stress and hope that you will always keep it in mind and realize that it is not necessary to have to suffer greatly in order to experience great peace in one's lifetime and be thoroughly appreciative of or grateful to the Power above.

It is true that you have been fortunate in your lifetime in having the worldly necessities provided you and that the opportunities arose without great penalties on your part and, therefore, possibly the failure to fully evaluate and appreciate them.

On the other hand, I must confess that you have accepted these worldly opportunities and goods in a realistic fashion and made the best of them to the extent of your ability to date.

I don't think because of these facts that you are an atheist or ever will be one, because I know that you know better and understand that there must be a Power greater than we earthly mortals enjoy. Otherwise, there would be no life.

I agree with you that a man who has no God is not an atheist but, more accurately, is a fool to a certain degree, not particularly because of his own mistakes or deliberations but because he has not had the full measure of opportunities to know why.

From your own statements, I know you understand that there must be a Heaven, Reincarnation, and a Divinity, and only through the years of greater wisdom can one hope to fully understand and appreciate this.

I can't agree with you that you should turn to the Deity only when everything around you is black and woeful. That would be a weakness, and, for that reason,

I think an open mind and a better understanding of the facts will eliminate any need for turning from weakness to strength, and by understanding and appreciation, a greater understanding must naturally result from greater strength.

In reading my speech which I gave at a luncheon before the Protestant Fund Campaign group, you failed to understand my point.

I did not advocate religious instruction in that sense, but I did advocate that the Lord's Prayer be recited by the teachers and students at the opening hour of every school day, from the first grade through and until one passes into the world beyond, because, as the years go on, you will find that every day will be a school day, for you will be learning something new each day. That goes with age if an open mind is kept.

I have the same feeling with reference to having the children recite the Lord's Prayer at the opening of every school day as I have by having them sing the National Anthem in order to open their minds to the value of both as the years go on.

It is further true that you were never given direct instructions from the Bible at home because I felt that the instruction received in your schooling would probably be more effective.

Furthermore, I think that once a person has a full

appreciation of the Deity or the Power Above, he can live his religion in a simpler manner every day of his life and, at the end of the day, can thank the Lord for the blessings bestowed upon him as I have from the time my Mother taught me the Lord's Prayer.

Love and best wishes.

As always,

Daddy

Mr. William Rickenbacker
Harvard University
Cambridge, Massachusetts

I had asked Dad about his ideas on religious instruction, granted that he had never taken his family to church, not pursued a course of religious study at home, nor asked the blessing at meals—all the standard external exercises. His last paragraph is true to the letter. For nigh unto eighty years he has knelt down and prayed every night.

★ ★ ★

Edward V. Rickenbacker
10 Rockefeller Plaza
New York 20

November 8, 1948
(Dict. November 7, 1948)

My dear Pal Bill:

I am certainly happy to receive your nice long letter of November 3 which makes up for the absence of the two weeks which I mentioned in my last communication.

Yes, all of the experts, including myself, were lulled to sleep by sweet nothings from the dopesters and prognosticators of what was going to happen on Election Day.

It is a good lesson for all of us, and I shall give you my reactions on why we failed during your visit over Thanksgiving because hindsight is always better than foresight and it is additional proof of the necessity of thinking through to a logical conclusion, which few people will take time or have the capacity to do.

I agree with your frugality. You are doing an exceptionally fine job of saving your money. All I want you to do, though, is use good judgment and not squeeze yourself out of the necessities that will be of value to you.

With reference to your becoming a teacher, scholar, historian, critic, or what not, surely that is something that will take a lot of thinking through on your part, as well as ours, and we will have plenty of time to discuss it pro and con during the Christmas Holidays.

Yes, I agree with you that Dewey will probably become a college president. On the other hand, I think that Harold Stassen will become the titular head of the Republican Party before 1952 rolls around for many reasons, which we can discuss when you are home.

In the meantime, my love and best wishes.

As always,

Daddy

Mr. William Rickenbacker
Harvard University
Cambridge 38, Massachusetts

Edward V. Rickenbacker
10 Rockefeller Plaza
New York 20

Christmas, 1948

My dear Pal Bill:

Christmas and the Holiday Season are again with us, and I am happy, as is Mother, that both of you boys will be with us during your Holiday vacation.

There is little that I can think of that either of you needs in the way of necessities that might be appropriate as a Christmas gift.

Consequently, my only thought, as always in the past, is of your future, with the hope that you are preparing yourself now to compete with the conditions with which you will be faced after leaving college and as the years roll by.

Therefore, I am again placing in your account Three Thousand Dollars worth of Government Savings Bonds which, in turn, if kept by you, will be worth Four Thousand Dollars in ten years.

All of this is with the hope of developing a nest

egg for you which you, in turn, will be qualified to enlarge and improve upon for your own sake and that of your family when the time comes.

The future, as always, has its black spots, as well as its bright ones, but unless you are qualified to judge the difference between the two, and take advantage of the opportunities offered by the bright spots, you will fall victim to the evils of the black spots as millions have and always will.

The black spots in the future, as I see them, consist primarily of a trend on the part of the majority of our people to expect something for nothing, or more for less, or to think in terms of the world owing them a living.

Frankly, the world never has, and never will, owe anyone who is mentally and physically fit a living, unless they are willing to work and work hard for it.

The world is your oyster and it lies within your power and yours alone to succeed or fail in proportion to your experience, knowledge, and the judgment that will come from both.

Consequently, may I again implore you to always remember that God helps those who help themselves, and with this reminder, may Christmas and the Holiday Season be a happy one for you, and the year of 1949 a further stepping stone to greater progress and accomplishment on your part.

Love and best wishes.

As always,

Daddy

Mr. William Rickenbacker
New York City, New York

★　　　★　　　★

Edward V. Rickenbacker
10 Rockefeller Center
New York 20

February 17, 1949

My dear Pal Bill:

Yes, I think you got by very well for book expense for the spring term, and if the amount on hand in your account does not carry you through, I know you will let me know.

With reference to your going to music school, I thought we have had a musical son in our family for many years past and hope we will continue to have by your own desire to keep your interest in music.

As for a profession, I think there are a lot of other things you would rather do in the long run and have music as a private and personal attribute for your own benefit and that of your friends and family.

What I need most now is a Director of Public Relations, a good lawyer, or a new President of Eastern Air Lines—all of them have an admirable future and would keep one eating regularly, but, of course, one has to prepare for any one of them or all of them.

I'll have a chance to visit with you on the subject when you come down for the car.

Love and best wishes.

As always,

Daddy

Mr. William F. Rickenbacker
Harvard University
Cambridge 38, Massachusetts

An anxious moment in a parent's life: the son is within a few months of graduating from college, and a career is to be settled upon. Law? Diplomacy? The airlines? Music? Literature? Scholarship?

★   ★   ★

MANHOOD

★　★　★

1949 -

With graduation from college in June 1949 and residence taken up again at home, Dad's letters ceased. I tried my hand, at Dad's suggestion, in the advertising business. Within a year we were at war again. I had enough time to pick up Russian and join the Air Force as a cadet in January 1951 . . .

January 11, 1951

My dear Son and Pal Bill:

With your departure to enter the military services of your country as a cadet in the Air Force of the United States of America, Mother and I hope that you will remember and follow a few of the simple rules of life which will be beneficial to you as time goes on.

Always remember that a million friends are worth more than a million dollars because if you have a million friends you will never need to worry about a million dollars.

Always be respectful to your superiors and elders as it is an acknowledgement of your capacity to appreciate the benefits acquired from experience.

117

This was evidenced by my answer to a query recently, "What advice can you give the younger generation, based on your greatest failure?" My answer was, "Failure to evaluate and understand the advice of my elders in my youth."

Naturally, modesty on the part of one who has been blessed with so many attributes as you in your limited years is a tribute to your good judgment.

Consideration of others at all times, be they right or wrong, is an acknowledgement of your own limitations.

Appreciation of acts of kindness and thoughtfulness will always make it possible for you to reciprocate in kind.

Never worry about protecting my name or my reputation. But always remember that it is your name you must protect and live with the balance of your life, which I am sure will be a constructive one as well as one of service to your fellow man.

Never fail to live up to the rules of the game, always play it in accordance with your knowledge and appreciation of the difference between right and wrong.

Always be a *good* soldier and not just a man in uniform.

Never try to impress other people with your superiority of knowledge, the latter of which you have been blessed with abundantly.

Never fail to remember that to have a strong and healthy mind you must first have a strong and healthy body.

Protect your body by limiting the abuses that go with every day life and you will automatically protect your mentality.

To become a good pilot and remain one never forget that an airplane is like a rattlesnake, you must keep your mind and eye on it constantly or it will bite you when you least expect it which could prove fatal.

Study the design, mechanics, and operation of your plane thoroughly and in detail.

Learn the detailed functioning and limitations of your plane, its accessories and its engines, and you will never abuse them to the degree that you will be the sufferer.

Learn to know and appreciate the mechanics who work on your plane and every unit of its operation because their appreciation of you at all times may mean the difference between a successful flight and one that is not.

Take advantage at all times, without interfering with your regular duties, to benefit through wholesome outdoor exercise such as golf at which you are very proficient.

For your peace of mind and emotional stability, play the piano when you feel the desire, when time permits, and when the opportunity is available.

Be certain to let your superior officer know the necessity to favor your left shoulder for some time to come in your daily exercises.

Make arrangements with the finance officer to have your checks sent to me in care of Eastern Air Lines, and I in turn will see that they are credited to your bank account, from which you may issue checks and will keep you advised of your balance.

Never hesitate to let me know if your requirements or needs exceed your earning power or bank balance.

By remaining strong physically and mentally remember you will be helping your country to develop the greatest and strongest air power in the world which is basically the salvation of this nation and the future of its people.

Always keep in mind the men at the head of the Kremlin only respect force and power.

Realize how blessed we of this land have been in

our 160 odd years of existence. We have not suffered the penalties of starvation for generations at a time as other peoples of other lands have done. Neither have we suffered destruction of our homes, institutions of learning, commerce and finance.

There have been many times when I have felt that our standard of living had grown beyond reasonable proportions because we as a people have failed to appreciate the fruits and value thereof, and have become slaves to the philosophy of getting more for less or something for nothing.

There is no doubt that this country and our civilization are on trial and the problems of the future may be God's way of making us suffer for our lack of appreciation of our way of life and the blessings bestowed on us by the Supreme Power.

While it is an axiom in life, and has been since the beginning of the world, that suffering is the greatest developer for expanding mentality, it could become a great penalty imposed on us for our faithlessness.

You are certain as the years go on to have many heartaches, headaches, trials, and tribulations but when the hour looks the darkest never lose faith in that Power Above.

With faith in the Power Above you will have faith in yourself. And because of your faith your call to God in Heaven for help if needed will never go unheeded, and will bring you back to us, your family, and your fellow man for greater service when peace among men shall reign again.

Love as always,

Daddy

★　　　★　　　★

Edward V. Rickenbacker
10 Rockefeller Plaza
New York 20

April 23, 1951

My dear Pal Bill:

It has been a wonderful inspiration to millions of Americans who have had the privilege of seeing and hearing General MacArthur since his return to his homeland with his good friends, and it proves how frustrated, confused, and mystified the American people have become during the last two decades through false and immoral leadership.

What they see in this great soldier statesman is a symbol of their hopes, ambitions, and moral necessities in their hour of bewilderment.

To me, it is an act of God that General MacArthur decided to make a martyr of himself in order to awaken the American people to the realities that they are facing. I hope God will give him the strength and courage to visit at least a hundred of the larger cities of the United States and their peoples and to carry the same hopes to them personally, that he has already carried to millions.

Naturally, all of us are happy about the possibilities of the ranch in Texas, and I look forward to many years of pleasure, health, and happiness through the opportunity to help build for both you and Dave something deeply rooted in the soil of this great land which you can build upon, benefit by, and develop for your family and yourself in the true traditions of the sound principles laid down by our forefathers, which have made this country great.

Won't you let me have your sincere reaction at an early date? Love and best wishes.

As always,

Daddy

Cadet William F. Rickenbacker
AD12333684
Unit P.O. #2, Box 1478
Randolph Field, Texas

*The ranch was about 3,000 acres of hill country, 90 miles north-
west of San Antonio, exquisitely suited to sport and pleasure,
but hardly economic. After several years of struggle, the Rickenbacker family had to admit we were not ranchers. The ranch is
now a jamboree ground for the Boy Scouts.*

★   ★   ★

Edward V. Rickenbacker
10 Rockefeller Plaza
New York 20

June 12, 1951

My dear Pal Bill:

I noticed the story in the morning's paper and
heard on the radio about eight jets crashing out in
Ohio during a mass flight from Dayton to Selfridge
Field, which looks to me like either mismanagement or
sabotage.

That is why I have always tried to impress upon
you the value of being friendly with your mechanics
and knowing the condition of your airplane before you
take it up. Always check it carefully, for the sooner you
get into the habit of it, the sooner it will be
commonplace for you to do it.

Furthermore, with so many young men who have
had no mechanical background, as you have had, or the
value of association of experience which I have tried to
impart to you, there is bound to be carelessness,
indifference, or accidents because of lack of
knowledge.

Therefore, whenever you are in the air, never
relax, always be on the alert mentally and visually.

Then you won't fall victim to someone else's carelessness, which some of the boys have and will continue to do because of the above mentioned facts.

If everything goes well, I hope to get down to Texas about July 26 for a couple of weeks, and naturally, want to be there when you get your wings and before your transfer to whatever station the program dictates.

At the same time, it will give me a chance to help get Dave started in the right way on the ranch, in spite of the fact that I don't know any more about Long Horns than he does, but I think I might learn a little quicker because of experience. He is going to have a big job handling the ranch efficiently and effectively, but I am satisfied he will accomplish it as we all want him to.

In the meantime, love and best wishes.

As always,

Daddy

Cadet William Rickenbacker
AD 12333684
Unit P.O. #2, Box 1478
Randolph Field, Texas

Edward V. Rickenbacker
10 Rockefeller Plaza
New York 20

June 18, 1951
(Dictated June 17)

My dear Pal Bill:

On our return from David's graduation, we found your wonderful Father's Day telegram, and I want you to know how much I appreciate it.

In the meantime, your letter also arrived, and I am delighted with the tremendous progress you are making and that you are really beginning to get the feel of the greatness of that ocean of air we are circulating in. But again, in night flying, more than day flying, your alertness is paramount from the time you get in your plane until you leave it.

It would be grand if the jet school opened nearby, as you hope for, but don't be disappointed because there are always difficulties in getting a new school started, whereas the school at Williams, should that be the ultimate destination, is well organized and the personnel are well qualified.

With love and best wishes, as always, and my best to Dave.

Daddy

Cadet William F. Rickenbacker
Unit Post Office No. 1
Box 1478
Randolph Field, Texas

"The feel of the greatness of that ocean of air . . . . " This is pilot-talk, pure and simple. To nonpilots it's a cliché, a piece of tawdry, without bone or meaning. For the men who know this feeling and share this love, it is the name of a certain ecstasy.

★　　　★　　　★

Edward V. Rickenbacker
Rickenbacker Ranch
Hunt, Kerr County, Texas

October 15, 1951

My dear Pal Bill:

First, I am going to answer your note with reference to Senator McCarthy and Jessup.

Frankly, they are trying to smear Senator McCarthy out of the picture, but I doubt very much whether they will, and I am sure they will not expel him from the Senate. As for Jessup, there is not much doubt that he and his cohorts, Latimore, and two others who have since died, were guilty of many of our problems today, as far as the Chinese Communists versus the Nationalists are concerned. In other words, it is a helluva mess. But the things have happened. They cannot be undone. Now, it is a case of making the best of a bad mess, which is very costly, as you well realize.

Your letter of September 16 to Mother covering our 29th anniversary embodies some very beautiful sentiments, and it is one that both of us will cherish the rest of our days.

I received your letter of October 8, which was

written on my birthday, and though it was a day or two late, I am none the less grateful for the beautiful thoughts expressed.

With love and best wishes, as always.

Daddy

Cadet William F. Rickenbacker
Cadet Detachment, Class 52-A
Reese Air Force Base
Lubbock, Texas

★ ★ ★

Edward V. Rickenbacker
Rickenbacker Ranch
Hunt, Kerr County, Texas

November 5, 1951

My dear Pal Bill:

We were delighted to receive your nice long letter of October 30, and glad to note that you are continuing to bank $80 a month, but more happy to hear that you are playing some golf and doing a bang up job of it. I am wondering who the unfortunate victim was when you played a 68. Was it a cadet, an officer, or a local citizen?

I note what you say about all cadets becoming second class [men] as of yesterday and that many of your classmates received some cadet rank from Sergeant to Major but you remained a buck private.

You must not forget that your record of lack of military aptitude at Randolph follows you around, and therefore you must make extraordinary effort to have it changed as time goes on. I think it is only fair to the service and to the uniform you wear that you make a business of looking like a soldier and acting like one, because you certainly cannot expect to become an officer to lead and direct men if you prove by your actions and dress that you cannot control your own passions and emotions. Make a business of it, Pal—it will prove worthy as time goes on and very valuable to you in later years.

I am delighted to hear and get your thinking insofar as your future is concerned. Journalism has tremendous possibilities for your general qualifications and is a good stepping stone, to say nothing of an opportunity to broaden your vision and make contacts with men who are doing the things worthwhile and otherwise for the time being.

I think when the time comes that you are free
from Military service—and I hope that will be within a
reasonable time—it might be advantageous to first get a
job on a paper like the New York Times as a reporter
to get the foundation of reporting on the best. Then,
join an organization such as the Kiplinger Agency,
which also is the best, but take it step by step for then
you will have prepared yourself to do the best job as
you move along.

Again, a reminder, don't forget that as long as you
are in the service, you have an obligation to
understand the part you are playing and to look and
act the part at all times for the benefit of all
concerned, but primarily your own good self.

With love and best wishes.

As always,

Daddy

Cadet William F. Rickenbacker
Cadet Detachment, Class 52-A
Reese Air Force Base
Lubbock, Texas

Edward V. Rickenbacker
Rickenbacker Ranch
Hunt, Kerr County, Texas

December 6, 1951

My dear Pal Bill:

What you say about choosing the B-29 instead of
the F-94 for your next step in your training is
interesting to say the least, and I agree to a degree
with your thinking.

However, I hope you did not let the influence of
the B-29 training school at Randolph interfere with
your good judgment and doing the thing that should be
done.

I agree that if you watch your step and handle the
B-29 as it should be—always seeing that your crew is
in A-1 shape, that the ship is in good condition, and
the mechanics are on your side—you will learn a lot
and have something in the way of multi-engine
operation on your side, because even though at the
moment you may be thinking along other lines, the day
may come when you would want to join Eastern Air
Lines and learn all about it, and eventually follow in

my footsteps. You could do it if you made up your mind, were realistic, and applied yourself.

Should they decide against your choice of the B-29 program at Randolph, do not be upset or disappointed, because they may have reasons unknown to you for wanting you to take up the F-94 program, and of course, they have that prerogative, as you must always remember.

I am sure that if it works out that way, you will follow the same interest and application that you have in the past and benefit accordingly.

I agree that the multi-engine training will eventually lead into multi-engine jet bombers, and that knowledge and experience could prove very valuable as time goes on.

Yes, times are changing for both Truman and Churchill. It is difficult to know what truth is these days when you read of the scandals taking place in Washington, and in practically all high government places. Time alone will cure it, plus men with fighting spirit and character behind them.

With love and best wishes and looking forward to seeing you shortly before Christmas.

As always,

Daddy

Cadet William F. Rickenbacker
Cadet Detachment, Class 52-A
Reese Air Force Base
Lubbock, Texas

The dream of a successor at Eastern Air Lines persisted long. It finally subsided after Laurance Rockefeller bought me a lunch in 1955 and inquired as to my interest in becoming EAL's eventual president. I confided that it was not my dearest ambition. Since then the air transport industry has managed to struggle along without me.

★   ★   ★

Edward V. Rickenbacker
Rickenbacker Ranch
Hunt, Kerr County, Texas

March 10, 1952

My dear Pal Bill:

I am certainly happy that you wore your uniform at Jack Trabucco's wedding and found out that there was nothing unusual about being in uniform publicly and the same thing applies to the dinner party at Denman's.

Surely, you are entitled to be justly proud of the privilege of wearing an officer's uniform in the United States Air Force because you worked hard to earn it and I can say to you frankly, one of the proudest moments in my life was the privilege of pinning your wings on at the graduation ceremonies at Lubbock, Texas.

I know you must have had a light heart after cleaning up all of your paper work, getting the letters properly filed and answered. It should be something to remember because it is a wonderful feeling to always be able to keep abreast of the work you have ahead of you, by doing it today, and not letting it accumulate for tomorrow because there is bound to be more on every tomorrow, and such a precision of effort helps you in every other way.

I note that you are pleased with the Long Beach Base and the friendly and cooperative attitude of those in command. And I am also glad to hear that the products of Douglas and North American are being ferried out of the Long Beach Airport.

Both are good products. But, make a business of getting their manuals and studying them in advance of any flying in order that you will be prepared to handle them and do not be in too big a hurry about ferrying as first pilot for the more co-pilot experience you get, the better first pilot you will be.

Since you are starting a new phase of your career which probably will take you to many parts of the world, be sure to keep a detailed diary of your daily activities for here too—you will be happy to have it in years to come.

I am glad you have enrolled in an advanced Russian course via correspondence from the University of California. It cannot help but be interesting and it is a good asset to have in your bank of knowledge—I mean the Russian Language and the people.

Now for a few of my own troubles. When I got back to New York the Port Authority had made the mistake of closing the Newark Airport and our boys had to get all the airplanes out in a matter of two hours.

They not only moved all of the schedules from Newark to La Guardia and Idlewild, with all the Super Constellations to Idlewild, but they did so with practically no confusion and very few late departures the morning of the 11th—a tribute to all of the kids, and they have continued to do a fine job ever since under difficult conditions.

We were finally able to work out a deal with Pan

American at La Guardia to use the Marine Hangar they have under lease which was idle. So we moved overnight all of our materials, supplies and parts from Newark to La Guardia and are supplying Idlewild now from La Guardia instead of Newark which was a headache.

Our employees are victims of this condition particularly those from Newark because it is a long, tedious drive to and from either La Guardia or Idlewild but they are not complaining because they have hopes that we may be able to work out the Newark problem at some future date which will mean returning there.

We were on the verge also a few days after my return of having La Guardia closed because of the people's hysterical wrath and the petty larceny of local politicians haranguing us as they were trying to make character with their constituents.

Almost immediately after the last National DC-6 crash the local Communists took up the hue and cry to close all New York airports and even distributed a letter-sized leaflet all over the Jersey area giving me unadulterated hell, blasting the many accidents, and the Wall Street gamblers and thieves who run the air lines. They even had the audacity to sign the leaflet at the bottom of the page "By the Communist Party of New Jersey."

In addition, the Daily Worker in their National Edition has been front-paging the closing of the airports all over the country or in all major cities which, of course, is right down their alley because if they could close the airports in 30 or 40 major cities, the boys in the Kremlin would probably give them all gold medals.

All interested parties, Port Authority, government bodies and air lines got together in a big meeting a day or two after I returned to analyze the problem and, unfortunately, it fell to my lot to be the only one to lay out a constructive program which, in turn, they all approved and then nominated me the chairman of the Air Transport Coordinating Committee.

This meant that I have been doing the great majority of the work and Eastern Air Lines is carrying the ball for the rest of the operators. However, we had to do it, in order to protect our own interests but it is shameful the way people can let "George" take care of their problems.

We met with 20 topside members of the industry and government bodies two days that week because there were two things that had to be done, in my opinion, quickly. One was to give the people something tangible to get their teeth into and eliminate or minimize the hysteria. Number two, make it so strong that it would take it off the front page of newspapers, who were in a measure using it for circulation getters.

Late Saturday night we finally arrived at a program of cutting 226 schedules from La Guardia distributing them to Idlewild, Westchester, Teterboro and MacArthur Airports.

We moved the International flights at La Guardia to Idlewild meaning Colonial between New York and Bermuda; Trans-Canada between New York and Montreal; American between New York and Toronto, and Pan American between La Guardia and Bermuda.

I got the military to eliminate their activities in this area, as well as the private fliers and the owners of corporation planes, and then put in a preferential runway system that the pilots and operators adhere to religiously. This program was to be completed by March 1 and was.

This gave us front page stories, that I hope you received, because I sent them, which did just what I hoped for. But, in the meantime, some home owners, inspired in the Newark area, have started suit against all the air lines operating in there.

I have to appear before Senator Johnson's committee in Washington this week; also before Congressman Beckworth's committee, who were designated to make a thorough investigation of the problem.

Then I have to go before the full Civil Aeronautics Board, and also see Secretary of Air Finletter—in other words, it will be a busy week, but I hope it will be a productive one.

We have had to move awfully fast at Idlewild by building two completely equipped nose hangars out of lumber to handle two Super Constellations in order to get the kids out of the rain and snow, and under cover.

We also had to set up a Quonset hut—50 by 100 feet—to handle operations supplies and stores, and to cover the ground equipment.

All in all the program will probably cost us in the neighborhood of half a million dollars for something that is only temporary— to say nothing of losing about 20% of our New York business that was generated through New Jersey. However, time will cure this, too, with a lot of hard and intelligent work.

Love and best wishes.

As always,

Daddy

Edward V. Rickenbacker
Rickenbacker Ranch
Hunt, Kerr County, Texas

March 20, 1952

My dear Pal Bill:

How nice to receive your letter of March 13 and what a lot of surprises it included!

First, the fact that you might start delivery almost any day of the T-6's and C-54's to different parts of the country. I am glad you had dinner with Bert Holloway and his wife. They are very nice people and Bert is a great admirer of yours.

As time goes on, I am sure you will find that being a teetotaler lends countenance, ability, and self assurance in your daily activities, and keeps your mind and imagination alert because your body and mind are in a healthier condition. (Of course, the question of saving the price of a cocktail is of vital importance too.)

Your description of your new apartment and its equipment, plus the baby grand piano, at the price you are getting it certainly intrigues me. You are likely to have a roommate any time, and it will be me.

Your statement that you might soon be checked out on jet fighters is a pleasant surprise, and I am sure it will be a great thrill, but remember they move a lot faster than those you have been accustomed to flying. Therefore, the mind and body reactions and coordination must be stepped up accordingly.

I hope you have written for your subscription to The New York Times, because you must keep abreast of the daily activities throughout the world, and the political revolution that seems to be taking place at this time here in this country. I mean the unexpected flush for the moment in favor of General Eisenhower versus Senator Taft.

You certainly are a frugal young man with a keen financial mentality in figuring out your budget and possible savings during the next three years. I am proud of you, and wish I had you at my elbow for a year or two because you would be of great help to me in the years to come and to your associates.

Love and best wishes.

As always,

Daddy

Lieutenant William F. Rickenbacker
3609 East First Street
Apartment 6
Long Beach, California

Edward V. Rickenbacker
Rickenbacker Ranch
Hunt, Kerr County, Texas

April 21, 1952

My dear Pal Bill:

First let me say that Mother and I were tickled pink when you called a few nights ago upon your return from Japan. Yours was a welcome voice and it made Mother extremely happy as you can understand.

I agree with your statement . . . that the Air Force offers to young pilots things they could not get anywhere else, such as responsibility for expensive equipment, the consequent sudden need for maturity and caution, relatively high pay considering one's youth and inexperience, travel, people, connections, et cetera. All of which I am glad you understand and appreciate, because it will be of multiple value to you as the years roll on.

As for your problems at the end of three years, I cannot quite agree with you. You will have been paid a relatively high salary but on the other hand, you have concentrated and given dollar value in return. All of which means that when you get out of the service you will have a much more substantial background than you would have had had you started out in a common fashion in business and worked at it through this same period. ·

I am sure that when you do get out you will not be a greenhorn looking for work because there will be many opportunities that will be attractive to you. The one I am hoping that you might be interested in as time goes on is to join me in Eastern where we can have a lot of fun together and you can be of great assistance and progress very rapidly.

I agree with you that there will be a lot of boys who will want to stay in because of the relative security they think they are going to get but I know that you are not that kind. Your ambitions, ability, and hopes for the future are much greater and will be fulfilled by you.

Yes, the tax problem is a shocking one and getting worse as time goes on, but I am happy to note that you are interested in this problem and have analyzed it so clearly for your own benefit.

All of which means you will be prepared to handle your own problems in a much more efficient and realistic fashion as time goes on.

Your judgment with reference to your overseas tour of duty makes a lot of sense. On the other hand, you never know just what the ideal combination is and you have to be governed to a degree by events as they take place. Yes, it is astonishing how many people— particularly young people—go through life without planning or thinking of their future. They live from day to day and of course, that is why there are so many people on the relief rolls of the country at the moment. When old age creeps up on them or they get married and have a family and sickness or misfortune overtakes them they are at a loss as to how to overcome these problems, and some one has to take care of them for them. That I know will never be your problem.

I am delighted you have been giving my thought of your joining Eastern consideration, perhaps as a pilot for a year and then as a helper to me, because I am sure that two or three years at my elbow will be of great help to you and a great relief to me as time goes on and will prepare you for most any sort of a problem that the future may present.

Surely you must take your time to think about it and analyze it from every angle because there is plenty of time to make up your mind.

We really are having some frustration, confusion, and complications coming out of Washington. The taking over of the steel industry by the President, just

146

because the companies would not give in to his Labor Management Board on the outlandish provisions of same to CIO leadership, is probably the worst thing that has happened to this country since its inception. If he can take over the steel industry for political purposes, he can take over any industry large or small and that is one of the dangers of having a lame-duck President in office and in command for another ten months. His vindictiveness will really show through on the surface.

The stock market has of course had its ups and downs. The general trend has been down for the past several weeks due to the news coming out of Washington which is not conducive to the American Way of Life. It smells to high Heaven of dictatorship and socialism.

As for Mr. Taft and General Eisenhower, it is going to be a battle. How the American people can accept a man without knowing what he is thinking is difficult for me to understand. The General has got all the New Deal Republicans supporting him as well as the fringe Democrats and what a menagerie that is. That in itself should be evidence to the American people that there is something radically wrong in Denmark.

All of the international bankers are for him, naturally, as well as the so-called "Western

Democracies" because they think they will get more
from him of what we have got left than they would
from Mr. Taft and I do not doubt that they are right.

Take care of yourself and be sure and let us hear
from you from time to time.

Love and best wishes.

As always,

Daddy

Lieutenant William F. Rickenbacker
3609 East First Street
Apartment 6
Long Beach, California

★   ★   ★

Edward V. Rickenbacker
Rickenbacker Ranch
Hunt, Kerr County, Texas

May 5, 1952

My dear Pal Bill:

We were delighted to receive your nice, long letter
of April 26 and I might add that your description of

your flight to Japan has been copied many times and sent to friends.

Now for your sleeping habits, of course you are the best judge of what is best but on the other hand, there are always certain habits that one gets depending upon their activities.

I, too, have difficulty putting in a full night because I never needed as much sleep as some people do. It is not uncommon for me to go to bed at 10 o'clock and get up at 2 o'clock or 4 o'clock and do a couple of hours work. Then maybe I might go back to bed for an hour or two and get up at seven—sometimes to stay up depending on the mental activity and the amount of work to be done.

Your analysis of the Bethlehem Steel Report and the demands being made on them by the Unions is realistic and particularly gratifying to me.

Of course, Mr. Truman has assumed authority and in the opinion of a great majority of businessmen, he had no right to. His blast at the Steel Industry and the Union from the White House on Saturday morning with the threat to get together or he would raise wages on Monday was happily stymied by the Supreme Court's decision to review the Constitutional validity of his seizure. At the same time they are preventing any increases in wages until their decision on the Constitutionality is made.

In other words, he didn't get away with his arrogance and threat which is a good thing. All I hope is that they follow through which will take probably two or three weeks.

Yes, I agree with you that the Steel workers today are many, many times better off than the poor devils in Korea who are living in trenches and getting maimed or killed. To say nothing of the fact that most pilots living in tents are getting less than the average steel worker. This is the result of the Democratic Party's original acceptance of labor racketeers' money to promote their 1932 campaign when they borrowed five hundred thousand dollars from John L. Lewis. Once in the clutches of an unsavory element, it is difficult to get out from under it, which is something to remember.

Your description of the orders and cancellations is typical but isn't it regrettable that with all the billions that have been spent by the Air Force that they didn't have an extra tail wheel around for a C-46? That, too, is typical of the military when they have more money than they know how to spend. Usually a great portion of it is wasted because of the lack of brains and organization.

The oil strike, as you no doubt realize by now, if you are in the country, is cutting all airline activities by thirty percent on Tuesday, April 6. Again, because of the manner in which the Unions and the bureaucrats in Washington have played the game.

I agree with you that it is probably advisable to accumulate cash for the time being rather than try to out-guess the Market or what is going to happen because of what Washington does. These are uncertain times and very frustrating and confusing, to say the least, for a business man.

Mother and I tried to phone you last night but could not reach you. We are going to try again this afternoon with the hope that we can find you in. Maybe you are in Japan by this time.

Love and best wishes as always,

Daddy

Lieutenant William F. Rickenbacker
3609 East First Street
Apartment 6
Long Beach, California

★   ★   ★

While on a military trip to the Philippines I came across the rumor that General MacArthur had made illegal (or large: in some minds the two are one) profits from the San Miguel brewery. Not wishing to undermine a good beer with an unsubstantiated rumor, I raised the question with Dad. Who, of course, went straight to the top . . .

Edward V. Rickenbacker
Rickenbacker Ranch
Hunt, Kerr County, Texas

June 3, 1952

My dear Pal Bill:

I am attaching a copy of General Courtney Whitney's letter which is self-explanatory.

Frankly, I would like to own a piece of that Philippine Brewery because any company that can afford to pay $35,000,000 in taxes is quite a company and I see no more reason for not owning a piece of it than not drinking the beer. It must be good beer.

I am cutting this letter short as I just got back from the interrogation at the Federal Grand Jury in Newark which is trying the three accidents in Elizabeth, New Jersey. It was about a two hour grind and now in another hour I will be on my way to Atlanta and then Athens, Georgia, where I am making the Commencement address tomorrow about noon. I will send you a copy of it and I would like to have your reaction when you get the time.

I will write you more fully over the weekend unless I am lucky enough to be able to get a break and get down to the Ranch for a week or ten days.

Love and best wishes.

As always,

Daddy

Lieutenant William F. Rickenbacker
3609 East First Street
Apartment 6
Long Beach, California

May 26, 1952

Dear Eddie:

I have your note of May 20, 1952.

Please inform your son, Bill, that General MacArthur has never had a dollar invested in any brewery or any other industrial venture in the Philippines. Like most of us who have been there, through the years, he has dabbled in some gold stocks, but other than this he has had no property ownership whatsoever.

This rumor that he has owned the San Miguel Brewery is a recurrent one, started I believe in World War II. It seems to me that it was either started or carried on by Drew Pearson as one of his typical smears against MacArthur, although I personally could never see what discredit might emanate from the alleged ownership of a corporation which has been so successful. As I recall, it has paid the Philippine Government over $35,000,000 a year in taxes. It is the leading corporation in the Philippines and, I believe, one of the most profitable ventures anywhere. As far as I know, the General did not even have so much as a glass of beer from this enterprise.

I hope this clarifies the matter.
With cordial regards, I am

Faithfully yours,

Courtney Whitney

Edward V. Rickenbacker
Rickenbacker Ranch
Hunt, Kerr County, Texas

July 16, 1952

My dear Pal Bill:

I am sorry Mother took the Eisenhower nomination
so badly but she, like everyone else, must realize that
politics are politics. They always have been and always
will be. All we can hope for is that the Lord will
endow Eisenhower and his team-mate, Senator Nixon,
with the sublime guidance needed to run this land of
ours the way it should be run.

Yes, we must stay and fight it through. It is our
only chance but it is a grand lesson particularly for a
young man because it will give you an idea of what to
expect and guard against as life rolls by.

I, too, am looking forward to a wonderful weekend
with you, Mother, and Dave, since I understand Brian
and Patty have gone home for a week or ten days.

I only wish I could be with you longer but then again the sooner you get your trip over with in the Pacific, the sooner you will be back home with us again.

Love and best wishes.

As always,

Daddy

Lieutenant William F. Rickenbacker
Rickenbacker Ranch
Hunt, Kerr County, Texas

It was many years more before I could understand that it was not necessarily hypocrisy to oppose a man in the primary, vote for him whilst holding one's nose, and then support him as a good American when President. All subsequent experience, not to mention the uproar in the streets today, points to this as the wisest course.

★   ★   ★

On duty near Seoul, Korea . . .

Edward V. Rickenbacker
Rickenbacker Ranch
Hunt, Kerr County, Texas

October 20, 1952

My dear Pal Bill:

First, let me apologize for my neglect in writing you during the last three weeks, in fact, it has been over thirty days.

Bob Lovett, Secretary of Defense asked me to make a trip for him which took ten days of high pressure visiting the Marine Corps' School at Quantico, Virginia, but they put on a realistic capture of a beachhead and their use of helicopters was a surprising demonstration, in fact, amazing, and the one great thing that came out of it was the individual training they give every man that joins the Marine Corps for his own individual security and collective security of the group. We went from there to Pensacola, Florida, where we boarded an aircraft carrier and saw the students come out to sea and land on the deck in their final checkout. It was a wonderful demonstration. Then we took a crash dive in a new Snorkel Submarine and got down about 150 feet under water for an hour or so. Then back to the carrier when the boys came out in a helicopter and picked me off the deck and took me in to talk to all their 2500 cadets, and that evening, before darkness, the Blue Angels put on a demonstration, that is a group of four Navy pilots, in Supersonic Jets that was truly amazing for precision flying.

From there we flew to Eglin Field, Florida, which is a large experimental station and saw all of the late models and prototypes of things to come. There I rode in a Jet T-33 and also a B-47, all of which, in a measure, is fantastic. It is at this station where they have a tremendous refrigerated hangar where they can simulate freezing conditions to 70 below zero for the whole hangar, which is a mammoth thing, or any department of it. It is hard to believe you could get those sort of temperatures when it was 100 degrees natural Fahrenheit on the outside.

We went from there to Fort Benning which is the Infantry Training School just outside of Columbus, Georgia, and this is truly amazing, particularly the training of the Airborne Troops. We also saw a tremendous demonstration of parachute drops en masse as well as cargo and weapons en masse including ten and one half trucks and hundred and five howitzer guns. Here too, individual training was stressed beyond expectation. In other words, everything proved that our men, with the proper training, could defeat any combination if we gave them the proper weapons in sufficient numbers and time which I hope God will forbid becoming necessary.

All in all, it was a wonderful ten days; I rode in three kinds of helicopters, an aircraft carrier, a submarine, two types of jet airplanes, took a simulated parachute drop from the tower and then rode in a Mark 47 Tank in a simulated battle. Of all of them, you can have the tank, but the surprising thing is that every man seemed to like his individual service that he is associated with better than any other, which of course is always a blessing.

As for the election, Mr. Truman has probably hit a new low in his campaigning for Stevenson. Never have I known a politician, let alone a President, get into the gutter so deeply. It didn't seem possible, but he is proving that he knows where he belongs and unfortunately, a lot of people believe him.

At the moment, it looks to me like a horse race, but anything can happen between now and then to switch the masses in their choice of candidates. My only hope is that it will be in Eisenhower's favor and of sufficient majority to sit the New Dealer's and all of their crooks down so hard that none of them will recover, at least in this generation.

With love and best wishes.

As always,

Daddy

2nd Lt. William F. Rickenbacker
A02222858, Box 73
21st Troop Carrier Squadron, Det. No. 1
APO 970 c/o Postmaster
San Francisco, California

★　　　★　　　★

Edward V. Rickenbacker
Rickenbacker Ranch
Hunt, Kerr County, Texas

October 30, 1952

My dear Pal Bill:

I am voting by absentee ballot in Texas, hoping it will do some good. I hope you have done the same because if Texas should go for Eisenhower, it would mean he would win by a good majority on November 4th. Right now it looks like a horse race. The polls give him a slight edge over Stevenson, but the mud is beginning to splatter in all directions. Truman has taken his high office into a new low in his attacks on the Republican Party and Eisenhower without truth or facts.

Mother said she had a letter from you enclosing some sketches which she was sending and I am looking forward to receiving it in Washington. In the meantime, I hope everything is going well with you and that you are not letting realism upset you, but holding on to your individuality within yourself and remembering always that a soldier, particularly an officer, must follow the rules of the game regardless of how hard it may be to take momentarily.

Try to keep in mind that it is not so bad when you look backwards because the future is always so bright.

With love and best wishes.

As always,

Daddy

Dear Pal [Handwritten P.S.]

I just read your last letter. Please don't refuse any medals regardless of what they are for. It won't help you while in the service to do so.

Love

Edward V. Rickenbacker
Rickenbacker Ranch
Hunt, Kerr County, Texas

November 6, 1952

My dear Pal Bill:

Well, it has come and gone. The election is over
and thank God we have a new President who has a
majority in the House and in the Senate. It was a
tremendous surprise to everybody. I mean the great
landslide and mandate, which is a mandate by the
people of this country.

I am attaching an editorial in the News and also a
map showing the states that went Eisenhower, which
you may have had before this.

I woke up the morning after the election with a
terrific load off my shoulders, because I had been
waiting and battling for twenty years to have such a
thing happen. In addition to the Democrats getting
badly licked, their little mouthpiece, in the form of
Truman, not only had the condemnation of all the

people who voted for Eisenhower, but he is now getting the blame from the rest of his cutthroats and supporters for having brought about the defeat of Stevenson with his whistlestops, which I am in favor of.

Actually, I feel as if America is back in the hands of Americans again, and to have Eisenhower crack the "Solid South" as he did, particularly our State of Texas, was the surprise of the ages. Now, we too, can be Americans in Texas.

I am leaving in the morning for the ranch and hope to stay there through Thanksgiving to get a much needed rest, and to help Dave in any of his problems. The next time you hear from me, it will be from the ranch.

With love and best wishes.

As always,

Daddy

Second Lieutenant William F. Rickenbacker
AO 2222858
21st Troop Carrier Squadron, Det. No. 1
APO 970, Care of Postmaster
San Francisco, California

Edward V. Rickenbacker
Rickenbacker Ranch
Hunt, Kerr County, Texas

November 26, 1952

My dear Pal Bill:

Well here I am, still enjoying the fresh air of
Texas, getting a lot of sleep and not too much exercise,
all on the day before Thanksgiving.

What you say about Eisenhower and the election is
true in a great measure, and I am sure that as time
goes on he will prove much better than a lot of people
anticipated. This is particularly true of his cabinet
appointments and his general soundness insofar as our
economic and political problems are concerned.

Evidence of this can be seen in the reaction of the
stock market during the last week, and I might add
that I telephoned Miss Shepherd this morning to buy
you 400 shares of Bethlehem Steel which is selling
around 52—300 shares of which will be repaid when I
sell your Eastern Air Lines stock. Selling your 650
shares of Eastern Air Lines should provide sufficient to
pay for 300 shares of Bethlehem.

It is good news to hear that your scheme for flying local at night has worked out so well and that you had the C-47 up several times on your own. Yes, it makes a difference when you are in command of a ship as compared with being co-pilot. The responsibilities alert and key you up to do a more perfect job.

I am glad to learn that the Scheduling Department now has you set up second in line to be checked out as an AC Aircraft Commander. I don't know what that means, but I assume that it means First Pilot. Of course, I am delighted that you are ready, willing, and able.

Your going on the water wagon on November 1st is an admirable action, not because of what it saves you but because of your health and the psychological influence on one of your tent mates. My heartiest congratulations! It displays a spirit of character that I have always known you had in abundance.

And now the responsibilities of being in command of a big bird and the lives of others will stand you in great stead. At a time in life when you are building a physical foundation, it will be lasting and valuable in emergencies in years to come. In a measure, I had the same experience when I went on the wagon when I was 19 and quit smoking for eight long years, to which I attribute my ability in later years to overcome the hazards of the accidents to which I fell victim.

Yes, I agree with you one thousand percent that the more knowledge you have of all branches of your service, the more capable and able you will be to perform your duties. Of course, it takes effort, but the more effort you expend the more knowledge you gain.

A man in command of an airplane with lives at stake, and to whom he is responsible, can never have too much knowledge or ability in case of an emergency.

I concur, too many pilots are airplane drivers. They know so little about the equipment or the technique of the different equipments that they should know all about in order to perform a man's job. But that is human nature and will always be so. It must be remembered that a man, like a nation, who works the hardest and most intelligently, cannot help but lead the other fellow, and God knows we need many more leaders in these trying times.

Your third from last paragraph makes Mother and me, as well as Dave and Patty, hold our breath because of the encouragement it gives us that you may be home in May or June instead of the late summer of 1953.

Yes, we will need you when the caterpillars are in the walnut trees next May or June because without you, I cannot do it alone. So guard yourself accordingly.

Everybody sends their love and best wishes, and God's blessings until we meet again.

As always,

Daddy

Second Lieutenant William F. Rickenbacker
A.O. 2222858
21st Troop Carrier Squadron
A.P.O. #970
Care of Postmaster
San Francisco, California

★   ★   ★

Edward V. Rickenbacker
Rickenbacker Ranch
Hunt, Kerr County, Texas

December 8, 1952

My dear Pal Bill:

We arrived home late last Sunday night, and I woke up Monday morning with a Flight Engineers strike on my hands which grounded all our

Constellations. It was a wild cat affair and illegal since the case was in mediation in spite of the fact that the contract had run out at midnight on November 30th.

To make a long story short, we wrote them on Monday night explaining the problem and the consequences of their action. On Tuesday night we wired them that unless they returned to work by 2 p.m. on Wednesday that they would be off the payroll, losing their seniority rights and service rights. None of them returned, the result being I sent out a call for Flight Engineers and started to train some of our mechanics who had gone through the ground course and all they needed was flight training. Within 48 hours we had received over 200 applications from all parts of the country from which we could readily screen 160, the total number of Flight Engineers on strike, or the total number that we have employed.

The mediator for the National Mediation Board was trying his best to get the boys back. The pilots refused to recognize the strike so we had several of our Super Constellation flights being operated with supervisory Flight Engineers, and within ten days to two weeks we would have been back in business, regardless of the strikers.

However, when they found out I meant business, they started crying like babies—the great majority of them pleading for the opportunity to come back.

Also, the mechanics refused to recognize the strike. Finally, on Friday evening they begged the mediator to plead with me to modify my position, which I finally did under certain conditions.

The conditions were that they would come back to work immediately without any reservations and on the same status that they left—wages and conditions—and after they were back on the job, we would then discuss further mediation. They were happy to agree to this. I hope it is a lesson they will never forget.

It is surprising how three or four ringleaders can make stupid asses out of 155 men or make them more stupid than they really are.

In the meantime, we have lost about a million and a quarter dollars in revenue.

All the Flight Engineers wanted was 85 per cent of the Captain's pay and the position of being second in command—this in view of the fact that I have spent an average of ten thousand dollars or more on most of them to train and have brought them up from helpers or apprentices through the years.

Can you imagine a Flight Engineer being second in command when the Co-pilot's obligation and duty is to fly the airplane if anything happens to the Captain? In addition, he has to prepare himself to become Captain. It doesn't make sense.

Now that Ike has been there [Korea] and is on his way home, a lot of people will think that everything has worked out satisfactorily, when in reality now the momentous decision must be made—what to do next.

With love and best wishes.

As always,

Daddy

Second Lieutenant William F. Rickenbacker
AO 2222858, Box 733
21st Troop Carrier Squadron, Det. No. 1
APO 970, Care of Postmaster
San Francisco, California

Edward V. Rickenbacker
Rickenbacker Ranch
Hunt, Kerr County, Texas

December 11, 1952

My dear Pal Bill:

You know that General MacArthur made a speech saying he had a plan to cure the Korean situation without great losses and without running the risk of involving us in an all-out World War III, and that General Eisenhower was big enough to cable him that he would like to discuss his plan and program with him on his return, which MacArthur graciously agreed to do.

This was a ten stroke on the part of both of them, which made the little man in the White House smaller, and now he is demanding that MacArthur come down and tell him all the details of the plan because the little man still claims to be the Commander-in-Chief—but only in his own estimation, in my opinion.

I don't think MacArthur will—and I hope he won't. But the editorial comment and the radio commentators' comment on Truman's demand have brought an avalanche of criticism, which in my opinion is justified and should continue to be increased because of the tactics he used.

Since the little man fired General MacArthur, he has never as much as seen him or asked for his advice, suggestions or recommendations. The true portrait of the size of a man, particularly in view of the great stature of General MacArthur and his known genius both military and statesmanwise and a lifelong record of service to his fellow men and country, is shown.

Such is Life. In the meantime, our love and best wishes.

As always,

Daddy

Second Lieutenant William F. Rickenbacker
AO 2222858, Box 733
21st Troop Carrier Squadron, Det. No. 1
APO 970, Care of Postmaster
San Francisco, California

Edward V. Rickenbacker
Rickenbacker Ranch
Hunt, Kerr County, Texas

December 22, 1952

My dear Pal Bill:

We were all delighted to receive your letter of December 8th and glad to know that you have been checked out as first officer and are now in command. Heartiest congratulations on a well deserved honor for which you have worked so hard.

Your description of your first flight as commanding officer of the ship is fascinating, to say the least, and of course, the experience with the hydraulic system and the landing gear is something that you must always remember can happen and as I have repeated so often through the years, never fail to be alert from the minute you take your seat in the ship until you get out of it. I am also happy to note that your knowledge of the mechanics of the ship helped you in this emergency.

More power to you for having volunteered for the emergency air evacuation to Hoengsong. But, here again, knowledge and alertness were on your side.

It seems unbelievable that there are only two of the artificial kidney machines in the world today. If they are good, they should have 10,000 of them and be working day and night to produce them, and not make it necessary to bring a youngster all the way from Japan to Seoul for treatment which I hope he received because the poor kid must have been in a terrible condition from your description.

Life is a cruel thing at times, and yet, I wonder whether the Power Above doesn't find it necessary at times to prove to us that we are not grateful for all of our blessings, or to make us appreciate them more.

Your decision to let the co-pilot, even though he was a greenhorn, fly the ship while you were prepared to take care of any emergencies, is good news to me because that shows you have the faculty of freezing up and really cold-bloodedly starting to think under trying circumstances. Again, my congratulations on the good judgment.

Your decision to jump back on the wagon after helping Ed Shaw celebrate his return to the States for discharge is again evidence of your mental capacity to control your physical wishes or desires. No one can successfully mix alcohol and gasoline and not run the risk of paying a terrible penalty sooner or later.

We are going to miss you, but God bless you, and enjoy the holidays as best you can.

As always,

Daddy

Lieutenant William F. Rickenbacker
AO 2222858 Box 733
6461st Troop Carrier, Squadron, Det. No. 1
APO 970, Care of Postmaster
San Francisco, California

★   ★   ★

Edward V. Rickenbacker
Rickenbacker Ranch
Hunt, Kerr County, Texas

January 26, 1953

My dear Pal Bill:

Pardon my delay in writing you during the past
week because I was on the West Coast with several of
my gang going over the jet air transport problems and
designs with Lockheed Aircraft Company, Douglas and
Boeing of Seattle.

Don't let your antagonism for the brass or the false

philosophies of the military get your goat. These have been in existence ever since military men existed, and probably will continue. Smile and make the best of it because you will have a greater peace of mind and be much more effective and efficient in your accomplishments.

Also remember that no matter how long you decide to stay in the Air Force, that when you leave you want to leave it with a clean record. And I am sure that by the time you do leave or your trick of duty runs out, you will have been promoted to a Captaincy which would be a fine thing historically to have a couple of Captains in the Rickenbacker family of different generations.

I had the good fortune of spending a day in Washington to see the Inauguration Ceremonies and the parade. I must confess that it was all well handled. President Ike made an excellent impression, the town was over-crowded and the parade was a magnificent thing. They even showed new atomic artillery pieces, which are a mammoth maze of complicated machinery, tremendously heavy and long. In fact, it had two distinct power plants—one at each end, synchronized with the other—so that they could get a balanced control, with two driving crews who synchronized each other's activities by telephone.

Everybody and his brother seemed to be there, and by the grace of the Lord it turned out to be a beautiful, mild, sunny day. A good omen, I hope, for the future.

Love and best wishes and God's blessing.

As always,

Daddy

Lieutenant William F. Rickenbacker
AO 2222858 Box 733
6461st Troop Carrier Squadron, Det. No. 1
APO 970, Care of Postmaster
San Francisco, California

Never did make Captain.

★　　　★　　　★

Edward V. Rickenbacker
Rickenbacker Ranch
Hunt, Kerr County, Texas

February 4, 1953

My dear Pal Bill:

Generally speaking, things are going along as well as can be expected. Eisenhower's speech on the state of the nation was very good. He didn't say too much, or, in my opinion, too little—sort of down the middle of the road.

Eastern Air Lines had its biggest month in history in January, and since March is, and always has been historically, the biggest month of every year, we expect this record to be broken substantially in March. But expenses have climbed proportionately and so have wages, which in the final analysis leaves us in about the same position we were. However, sooner or later, there has to be a leveling off of both prices and wages or we are sure to run into trouble because indications are that business will start declining this Fall, maybe sooner, and the Year of 1954 will be 10 to 15 per cent less with the possibility of going further in 1955 before a turn in the road comes. I hope I am wrong, but every indication points this way for the next several years.

We must not forget that we have been living on our surpluses and the fat of the land for the last 12 to

13 years, and these conditions cannot go on indefinitely. Along this line we will find ourselves without surpluses because of our deficit spending and our lack of a balanced budget.

Evidence of this future exists in the fact that farm prices in general and beef prices in particular have dropped down to below the pre-Korean period. Naturally, the farmers are yelling to High Heaven, or will be if the decline is not arrested. It may become contagious and spread to other lines before the normal law of supply and demand takes hold or should take hold.

Just what Mr. Eisenhower's decision on the Formosa fleet will mean to the future of the war in Asia is difficult to say. But as he says, it does not make sense to protect the Chinese Communists from the Chinese Nationalists when the Communists are our enemy. All in all, there has been a great deal of confidence inspired by the new Administration, and I hope it continues.

God bless you and we send our every best wish and our love.

As always,

Daddy

First Lieutenant William F. Rickenbacker
AO 2222858 Box 733
6461st Troop Carrier Squadron, Det. No. 1
APO 970, Care of Postmaster
San Francisco, California

★   ★   ★

Edward V. Rickenbacker
Rickenbacker Ranch
Hunt, Kerr County, Texas

February 9, 1953

My dear Pal Bill:

Again a Sunday morning at the office to be sure
that I am cleaned up as near as I can be since I am
leaving on Wednesday morning to go to Texas, where,
as I stated before, I have five speeches to make.
Mother and I are going to Miami after that.

Mr. Eisenhower is certainly moving up on the
problems that have accumulated over the last 20 years

of New Deal, Fair Deal, and Freakish Deal governments.

His latest move to eliminate wage and price controls is a good one, I believe, because I think the law of supply and demand will take care of matters in a characteristic American fashion, as they should.

I think his move to help the Chinese Nationalists on Formosa to help themselves is a good one, providing we give them airplanes to knock out the railroad from Mukden to Indo-China, because that will help the French and automatically dilute the Communists in North Korea, providing they also blockade the China coast, and keep our friends and black marketeers from running war materials and ammunition and weapons to our enemies.

Mr. Dulles' hurried trip through Europe and the positive manner in which he has approached the problems of telling them to help themselves if they wish us to continue to help them is going to do a lot of good I think, both practically and psychologically, in this cold war with the Kremlin.

Our old friend Steve Hannagan, who was on a trip through South Africa for the Coca Cola people, died of a heart attack in Nairobi, South Africa, a few days ago, and naturally it was very unexpected. It was a terrible blow because he is only 53 years old and never had shown any signs of heart trouble until the end.

Being a friend of 40 years, and having a more or less father-and-son-relationship, I naturally feel his leaving very keenly. But time marches on and unfortunately his body will not arrive here until next Tuesday or Wednesday, when I will be gone and unable to pay my last respects to the remains. But here too, time marches on.

May the good Lord continue to bless you, and with love and best wishes from all.

As always,

Daddy

Lieutenant William F. Rickenbacker
AO 2222858 Box 733
6461st Troop Carrier Squadron, Det. No. 1
APO 970, Care of Postmaster
San Francisco, California

Edward V. Rickenbacker
Rickenbacker Ranch
Hunt, Kerr County, Texas

March 13, 1953

My dear Pal Bill:

In answer to your letter of February 21st, I think you were very wise to go to the hospital and get your respiratory diseases cleared up because it's bad business flying with a cold. That's how I developed a mastoid in World War I and, as you say, it gives you a chance to rest, relax, and answer a lot of your mail.

Your analysis of Eisenhower's action in removing the 7th Fleet from the waters between Formosa and China is very good indeed. The only thing I could add is that we should give the Chinese Nationalists the necessary destroyers or other ships that would permit them to do it instead of our boys doing it. It would be a similar case to our lend-leasing to the British fifty destroyers prior to our entrance into World War II.

In addition, if we gave them some of our old fighter bombers and taught them how to use them, they could very easily cut the main railroad between Mukden, Manchuria, and Indo-China which has been supplying the Commies in Indo-China. It would save the French thousands of lives and our taxpayers billions of dollars.

I agree with you that Red China has already declared war on America and there is nothing that we could lose or they could gain by any formal declaration.

Now that Stalin is dead, it is my hope that the leaders in Moscow will get fighting among themselves for power and thereby bring about internal revolution in Russia. Let them kill each other and I think it will bring about peace for a long time to come. Of course, I realize that's wishful thinking but it has happened in history several times. Furthermore, it may have a salutary effect on Chinese Commie leaders and this may be an opportunity to break them away from the Russian regime. It also may be an opportunity to break the satellite countries away from Moscow because by the time they build up another leader with a halo around him such as Stalin has had the past three decades, a lot of things could happen.

Your analysis of Russia's advantages in the West and the fact that they've never been conquered from that direction, but have been conquered and overrun three different times in history from the East, makes a lot of sense. Of course, with the State Department being Communistic the past twenty years, it's readily understandable why they agree with the British who also have been Communistically inclined to throw our money and men into Western Europe. I think General MacArthur understands that situation better than any man living.

I agree with you that there are millions of Chinese who would go to work if Chiang Kai-Shek were given the go-ahead and got a "foothold" on the mainland. This certainly would confuse and upset the Chinese Commie leaders, such as Mao. Sooner or later it would bring about disagreement between Moscow and the Chinese Commies and help the situation in general.

Thanks for the article with reference to my speech at Austin, Texas, before the Joint Session of the Legislature of Texas. There's no doubt but what there still are a lot of sly and slick writers with Communistic tendencies attached to the Stars and Stripes, as there have been for the past twenty years and who must be cleared out.

We have also had an inquiry from the International News Service. They want to get up a story and try to make a full page of pictures for their Sunday supplement section which is sent all over the country. In other words, the ball is beginning to roll, and now it's a case of developing the herd of deer so that we'll have ample supply for the hunters.

Love and best wishes.

As always,

Daddy

First Lieutenant William F. Rickenbacker
AO 2222858 Box 733
6461st Troop Carrier Squadron, Det. No. 1
APO 970, c/o Postmaster
San Francisco, California

It still seems correct that if we had cut the Communist supply lines into Southeast Asia twenty years ago, we would have been spared the long agony of the Vietnam War. To urge such a thing was called warmongering, at the time. Nevertheless it would have served the cause of peace far more than the policies we actually followed.

★ ★ ★

Back in the States, now, and by the greatest good luck stationed in San Antonio, less than two hours' drive from the ranch.

Edward V. Rickenbacker
Rickenbacker Ranch
Hunt, Kerr County, Texas

July 31, 1953

My dear Pal Bill:

I am glad to note that you have been checked out as a first pilot and from what Mother has told me of your description, I am anxious to hear it, too, at the first opportunity I get because I am sure you did a good job.

You will have a grand time with the pilots returning from the Troop Carrier Squadron, who will be based with you. It will be a lot of fun reminiscing of the days gone by.

Now that the truce is signed, I hope they can develop it into a real armistice and peace pact with permanency—not only in Korea, but the world over. Unfortunately, I am a sceptic and, knowing the Russians and the gullibility of our own negotiators and government heads, it looks to me as if we are being taken for a giant sleigh ride in the middle of the summer.

I have just heard of the death of Robert Taft at 11:30 A.M. today. This is a terrible loss to the country as a whole and, particularly, to the President and his associates. Never in the history of the country have we needed his type of balanced thinking and knowledge of our problems as we need it now. But the Good Lord has willed otherwise. Let's hope for the best.

It seems ironical that he should have been defeated but, on the other hand, it may have been the defeat that brought about this condition because success distributes the adrenalin in a man's body to the degree that it corrects many illnesses and weaknesses. His defeat may have brought about his illness or hastened its development. Who knows?

Again, I say we can only hope that it is all for the best but we do know that we have lost a great leader, a great statesman, and, above all, a great man.

Love and best wishes.

As always,

Daddy

Edward V. Rickenbacker
Rickenbacker Ranch
Hunt, Kerr County, Texas

New York City
January 16, 1954
(Dictated 1/13/54)

My dear Pal Bill:

Last evening I returned after a rather interesting trip to Washington. On Monday night I had dinner at the White House with fourteen other men, as guests of the President at one of his usual stag dinners.

On arrival at 7:30 P.M., we were ushered into where they were having cocktails and a general discussion was being held and at 8:30 we sat down to dinner.

To name a few of the guests—I was across the table from the President and next to Dr. Mayo, head of the Mayo clinic at Rochester, Minnesota. Also present were Mr. Ernest Weir, Chairman of the Board of the National Steel Company in Pittsburgh, Mr. Charles

White, President of the Republic Steel Company, Cleveland, Ohio, Mr. Jack Knight, Publisher of the Miami Herald, the Akron Beacon News, Detroit Free Press, and the Chicago Daily News, and many other men of the same caliber, including the Chief Counsel of the Pillsbury Flour Company in Minneapolis, who originated the Eisenhower write-in campaign during the primaries and started the bandwagon rolling for the nomination.

An interesting discussion followed and after dinner we retired for coffee and cordials. Of course, I was on the wagon. Many subjects were brought up and I am sure that you would have had a tremendous thrill in hearing the pros and cons, had you been there.

Also, I forgot to mention above that Bob Kleberg, head of the King Ranch in Texas, was present and said he wanted to come to the Ranch some day and have a visit. He is a brother of my good friend, Dick, who was a Congressman in Washington for many years.

The discussion lasted until 11:00 P.M.—longer by an hour than is normal for these occasions but the President was at his best and seemed to be enjoying the evening tremendously. In fact, he admitted that it was the best party that he had had to date. He looks fine and seems to be in good shape.

As you know, I was presented with the Big Brother Award of the Big Brother Movement. The purpose of this 50 year old organization is for men in all walks of life to act as big brothers, on a personal basis, for maladjusted youngsters. I have done this and been tremendously pleased with the results. Also, last year I headed up a campaign for funds which was very successful.

They arranged for President Eisenhower to make the presentation at the White House on Tuesday at 2:00 P.M. The Executive Committee, made up of 14 members of the Big Brother Movement, came from all parts of the country to be present.

Here again, the President was very jovial and seemed delighted to have the chance to make the presentation. Of course, there were a million photographs and movies taken during the occasion and I shall have a collection of them, which I shall show you all.

In other words, now I am back in the salt mines with my nose to the grindstone after flirting with the President and the White House for two days in succession.

I am sending my place card from the White House with the emblem and also a knife which all of the guests received from a Mr. Frank Wood, through the President, as well as the card which was attached. Also, there was a penny with the knife but we had to give the penny back to the President in order to prevent the cutting of the friendship. I think Mother could well afford to put these in the little chest as keepsakes.

Also, I shall send you two packages of matches with the White House emblem and President Eisenhower's name for you and Dave as keepsakes.

My love and best wishes to all.

As always,

Daddy

Lieutenant William F. Rickenbacker
Rickenbacker Ranch
Hunt, Kerr County, Texas

No doubt about it, Ike was magnetic. I had met him once or twice in 1949 and felt the radiations. Dinner at the White House might very well have converted me too. So Pillsbury was the villain, hm?

★　　　★　　　★

Edward V. Rickenbacker
Rickenbacker Ranch
Hunt, Kerr County, Texas

New York City
July 6, 1955

My dear Pal Bill:

It was nice of you to call us the other evening and I enjoyed the visit on the telephone. Naturally, Mother enjoyed talking with both Sandy and yourself.

I am also happy to note that you have been able to work it out satisfactorily with your boss to have about nine or ten days for your honeymoon, and it will be a wonderful thing for both of you.

As for setting the wedding date on September 3; that is going to work out very well for Mother and me because we can leave on Sunday and I can spend a week at the Ranch providing conditions permit, which I never know as you well understand from past experience.

Now with reference to your thinking covering the

guaranteed annual wage subject, I agree with you 100 per cent that it is a bad one, and we will have to learn to live with it.

Unfortunately, as you say, over the years we have developed this absolute security idea with all of our give-away programs.

Of course, I agree further with you that the public do not want to think of their own welfare or plan it. They want more and more of it to be done by the government or industry, and someday they will wake up and find themselves with a planned economy that practically equals a positive dictatorship insofar as their opportunities and privileges are concerned. Such are the weaknesses of human beings.

Yes, I agree with you that the automobile industry has a difficult problem and one that I see no way of curing because as long as we have the free enterprise system and competitive effort all of them are going to try to be first.

Therefore, they usually all come out together with their new models normally in the late fall or early winter and there is where the rub is. Everybody is anxious to be first and, of course, the public is always interested in buying the latest.

Unfortunately, Bill, the free enterprise system and

the competitive system make it almost impossible to set up a pool of labor which could be used and distributed over the industry because about half of the components used by the automobile companies are produced in many states by small concerns in spite of the fact that the major part of the industry is located in Detroit.

Therefore, such a pool or concentration would automatically disrupt the economy of many communities and would not be tolerated under any circumstances by the labor racketeers.

In addition to the labor racketeers not agreeing to such a program, naturally, the manufacturers would not nor would the industry.

Yes, I agree with you that everybody is crying or applauding about the guaranteed annual wage, and though it does not show on the surface I can assure you that there has been some very deep thought given this matter by the heads of the big companies. I will tell you about a conversation I had with Harlow Curtice, President of General Motors, on my return flight from Indianapolis when I see you.

I further agree with you wholeheartedly that government and industry are in a measure to blame for this present philosophy originated by President Roosevelt during his four terms.

Of course, all politicians want to be in office and

the only way for them to get into power is to promise everything under the sun from the cradle to the grave to get the great majority of the common peoples' vote.

Then after they get in they want to remain in and in order to do that they have to keep giving more and more in spite of their own personal wishes or interests, all of which means to me that someday inflation will run rampant and none of us will have anything left because the dollar will be worth nothing.

That is why equities and land or material things are essentially a part of every portfolio instead of plain cash as we know it today.

In other words, cycles come and go, individuals go broke and succeed, corporations do the same, nations have always done it and will continue to do so, and until the public really suffers for their greed and selfishness they will learn nothing.

That suffering will be universal and could someday place us in the same position that China or India is in today or many of the other backward countries that once stood out as shining lights to the world such as Greece, Rome and Spain as well as France. Unfortunately, people never learn without suffering. They do not go to church until they are either sick, broke or in some other unfortunate misery. Then all human beings start crying for help, but when things are going good and they are riding the crest of the waves, as they are today in this country, the Power Above means nothing to them because the great majority are enjoying their blessings but have never earned them.

Generations previously laid a foundation and made it possible for them to have what they do. Consequently, they do not appreciate them and must someday pay a heavy penalty to learn how. Then they will go back to work again as other generations have in centuries gone by.

Do not be discouraged with my reactions to your thinking, but as you say you are sort of a visionary and that is good because it keeps you looking ahead and thinking through, which so few people today can do, and to me the best part of your whole letter is the fact that you have been thinking about this national problem that is going to affect everybody's pocketbook eventually.

Also, do not ever be discouraged about any thoughts you have not appealing to some people. Take it in your stride and keep thinking because if you get one good one out of a hundred you are fortunate.

I hope you will always ask for my advice or help in any of your difficult moments as long as I am around to give it, not that it will always be the correct answer but it helps to balance your own judgment and that is true of all of us.

Love to Sandy and yourself.

As always,

Daddy

Mr. William F. Rickenbacker
450 East 63rd Street
New York, New York

★   ★   ★

Edward V. Rickenbacker
10 Rockefeller Plaza
New York 20

Christmas, 1960

My dear Pal Bill:

Now that the shouting and the fireworks that covered one of the most bitterly contested presidential campaigns in the history of America, are behind us, I sit here on this Thanksgiving Day trying to remember the many good things for which my family and I are thankful.

It is a beautiful Thanksgiving morning in New York City. The sun is bright; the air is crisp, and Mrs. Rickenbacker and I are blessed with the opportunity of later joining our son and his family for a Thanksgiving dinner in the country.

As I think of the "cold" war, and the hearts that are bleeding for many peoples around the world, I realize that we Americans, above all other peoples, have been blessed with freedoms, opportunities and the individual dignity of man.

We Americans have an abundance of all the necessities of life, particularly food of all kinds, and when we think of the many peoples throughout the world, who are hungry on this blessed day, we should give thanks to the good Lord for having been born in this land where our brilliant forefathers had the courage and ability to write these blessings and freedoms into the Declaration of Independence and the Constitution of these United States which, unfortunately, too many have never read nor remembered.

I think of the birth of Christ who brought to earth the realization and understanding that all men should be free—free to worship as they see fit—free to work where they see fit—free to own their own homes—free to vote for whom they please—and above all, free to earn and save for the benefit of their old age and their children's future.

Then I realize that without the birth of Christ there never would have been the birth of our nation—a free America—whose moral obligation is to stand as a living example to the rest of the world of what freedom-loving people can accomplish in the short period of some 185 tumultuous years, and as a guiding star for others to follow.

Though the election of our new President for the next four years showed that the people were divided almost evenly in their choice between the two men, it is now the duty and obligation of every one of us to unite and merge behind our new President for the benefit of all, in order that this nation may continue to prosper so that we may continue to serve and lend a helping hand whenever and wherever needed.

In this spirit, let us all look forward to the approach of another Happy Christmas and Holiday Season, followed by a New Year which I hope will bring to you and yours the continued blessings you have enjoyed in the past, together with good health and happiness.

Most sincerely,

Daddy

Mr. William F. Rickenbacker
Briarcliff Manor, New York

Edward V. Rickenbacker
45 Rockefeller Plaza
New York 10020

August 11, 1965

My dear Pal Bill:

Miss Shepherd and I were up to the warehouse last week where we have a room full of everything under the sun, and in going over most of it, I found your personal letters to Mother and me during the years gone by.

After reading them over, I am sure the day will come when you will want to read them, as I know they will bring back many memories of yesteryears and you will be amazed at some of them.

I have these letters in my office, and as I recommend that you save them for your own future, as well as that of your youngsters because they, too, will benefit, may I suggest you drop by some day and pick them up.

Love and best wishes to all.

As always,

Daddy

Mr. W.F. Rickenbacker
Briarcliff Manor, New York

I am past redemption now, but perhaps my sons can be saved.

★　　　★　　　★

Synchronism

Capt. E.V.R.	W.F.R.
1922 marriage residence: Detroit	
1927 Rickenbacker Motor Company fails; head of Indianapolis Speedway	
1928 V.P. General Motors	born
1931 residence: Bronxville, New York	
1932 Medal of Honor	
1934 President, Eastern Air Lines	
1936	first place, Steinway competition
1937	residence: Irving School, Tarrytown,New York
1938 residence: New York City	
1939	residence: Asheville School, North Carolina
1940	ranking scholar, lower forms English prize
1941 travels for the War Department the Atlanta crash	ranking scholar Latin prize French prize
1942 adrift in the Pacific *Seven Came Through*	
1943 "Captain Eddie"; a film	French prize
1945	Spanish prize, mathematics prize first solo piano recital graduation *cum laude* residence: Harvard College

1946-1949		"H" for swimming (1946) and golf (1946 through 1949, captain '49) English, German, Greek graduation *cum laude* assorted local golf championships
1949-1950		advertising; Russian
1951-1955		Air Force pilot; advanced Russian composition; corporate accounting residences: Texas, Korea
1955		marriage; investment banking residence: New York
1958		son, Jamie
1960		submitted first article to *National Review;* associate editor, *National Review*
1961		son, Tommy; senior editor, *National Review*
1965	retirement from Eastern Air Lines *Fighting the Flying Circus* (reissue)	
1966		*Wooden Nickels*
1967	*Rickenbacker: An Autobiography* (#1 best seller, Jan. 1968)	
1968		*Death of the Dollar*
1969	*Rickenbacker* (paperback)	resigned from *National Review* to establish *The Rickenbacker Report* (weekly investment report)
1970		*Death of the Dollar* (paperback) *From Father to Son*